柔軟的力量（增訂版）

我選擇逆流而行，重新連結台灣與全世界

———————

邱月香　著

【BizPro】2AB537X

柔軟的力量（增訂版）
我選擇逆流而行，重新連結台灣與全世界

作　　　者　邱月香
採 訪 撰 稿　王淳美、吳鴻
編　　　輯　曾曉玲
內 文 設 計　江麗姿
封 面 設 計　兒日
行 銷 企 劃　辛政遠、楊惠潔

總　編　輯　姚蜀芸
副　社　長　黃錫鉉
總　經　理　吳濱伶
發　行　人　何飛鵬
出　　　版　電腦人文化

發　　　行　城邦文化事業股份有限公司
　　　　　　歡迎光臨城邦讀書花園
　　　　　　網址：www.cite.com.tw

香港發行所　城邦（香港）出版集團有限公司
　　　　　　香港灣仔駱克道 193 號東超商業中心 1 樓
　　　　　　電話：(852) 25086231
　　　　　　傳真：(852) 25789337
　　　　　　E-mail：hkcite@biznetvigator.com

馬新發行所　城邦（馬新）出版集團
　　　　　　Cite (M) Sdn Bhd
　　　　　　41, Jalan Radin Anum, Bandar Baru Sri
　　　　　　Petaling, 57000 Kuala Lumpur, Malaysia.
　　　　　　電話：(603) 90578822
　　　　　　傳真：(603) 90576622
　　　　　　E-mail：cite@cite.com.my

印　　　刷　凱林彩印股份有限公司
　　　　　　2019 年（民 108）6 月二版一刷
　　　　　　Printed in Taiwan
　　　　　　471-770-209-662-5
定　　　價　350 元

如何與我們聯絡：
1. 若您需要劃撥購書，請利用以下郵撥帳號：
郵撥帳號：19863813　戶名：書虫股份有限公司

2. 若書籍外觀有破損、缺頁、裝釘錯誤等不完整現象，想要換書、退書，或您有大量購書的需求服務，都請與客服中心聯繫。

客戶服務中心
地址：10483 台北市中山區民生東路二段 141 號 B1
服務電話：(02) 2500-7718、(02) 2500-7719
服務時間：週一至週五 9：30 ～ 18：00
24 小時傳真專線：(02) 2500-1990 ～ 3
E-mail：service@readingclub.com.tw

※ 詢問書籍問題前，請註明您所購買的書名及書號，以及在哪一頁有問題，以便我們能加快處理速度為您服務。

※ 我們的回答範圍，恕僅限書籍本身問題及內容撰寫不清楚的地方，關於軟體、硬體本身的問題及衍生的操作狀況，請向原廠商洽詢處理。

※ 廠商合作、作者投稿、讀者意見回饋，請至：
FB 粉絲團：http://www.facebook.com/InnoFair
Email 信箱：ifbook@hmg.com.tw

國家圖書館出版品預行編目資料

柔軟的力量 / 邱月香著 . -- 初版 -- 臺北市；
電腦人文化出版；城邦文化發行，民 107.12
面；　公分

　　ISBN 978-957-2049-05-1（平裝）
　　1. 邱月香 2. 傳記

783.3886　　　　　　　　　　　　107015546

1.1998 年邱月香參加環太平洋私校教育會議上台致詞 | 2. 擔任扶輪社社長的邱月香與丈夫合影 | 3.1994 年邱月香與媽媽生日宴上合影 | 4.2001 年參加扶輪社 GSE 獲頒市民榮譽之鑰 | 5.2016 年 ASOCIO 緬甸大會邱月香上台致詞 | 6.2016 年 ASOCIO 緬甸大會邱月香擔任與談人

7.2017 年邱月香致贈紀念品給馬來西亞當地 ICT 產業領袖 PETRONAS 會長 Tan Sri Sidek Hassan（左二）。ASOCIO 會長 David Wong（右二）、Pikom 副主席甘尼斯古馬（右一）| 8.2017 年巴西 WCIT 會議與斯里蘭卡簽 MOU | 9.2017 年與孟加拉部長 Zunaid Ahmed Pakal（右三）合影 | 10.2017 年 6 月與蒙古議長 Mr. ENKHBAYAR Jadamba, Member of the State Great Hural(Parliament) of Mongolia 合影 | 11.2017 年邱月香拜會亞美尼亞交通暨科技部長 Mr.Vahan Martirosyan | 12.2017 年邱月香參加孟加拉當地民俗婚禮 | 13.2017 年邱會長在美國華盛頓總部與 WITSA 幹部合影

14.2018 年 1 月在印度記者會上，與印度泰倫加納省資訊科技廳長拉奧 K.T. Rama Rao（右二）、NASSCOM 會長 Mr. Chandrashekhar（右一）合影｜15.2018 年 1 月邱月香與寮國當地協會理事長（左一）、部長（右二）與 ASOCIO 會長 David Wong（右一）合影｜16.2018 年 2 月邱月香與印度海德拉巴市機要秘書 Mr.Jayesh（左一）、WCIT2018 科技部部長 K.T. Rama Rao（左二）、NASSCOM 會長 Mr. R. Chandrashekhar（左三）、中華軟協任務分組國際主委黃旭宏理事（右一）合影｜17 2018 月 2 月 21 日 WCIT 閉幕式中，將下一屆主持棒交給亞美尼亞 WCIT2019 於 10 月在首都葉里溫舉辦｜18 2018 年 4 月瑞士日內瓦 WITSA 與 ITU 簽 MOU｜19.2018 年 4 月菲律賓商會來訪中華軟協

20.2018 年 5 月邱月香與泰國童振源大使（左）和泰國 ATCI 協會前理事長 Bunrak Saraggananda（右）合影｜ 21.2018 年 6 月邱月香與不丹資通部長 Lyonpo D.N. Dungyel（左）、ASOCIO 會長 David Wong（右）合影｜ 22.2018 年 6 月克羅埃西亞經濟商會（CCE）副會長 Mr. Ivan Barbaric（左二）及歐台工商聯合會（EBAT）總經理 Mr. Goran Gasparac（右一）拜訪邱月香｜ 23.2018 年 7 月邱月香應邀前往新加坡「區塊鏈論壇」致詞｜ 24.2018 年 8 月 WITSA 與美國 Resource America 簽 MOU｜ 25.2018 年 8 月跟 Goodwill 前 CEO Jim Gibbons（右二）請益：如何用數位化來幫助殘障者的需求

緣起

　　在 2017 年 9 月 10 日，超過 4,500 位資訊科技界的領袖和專家，從全世界 83 個國家，不遠千里、風塵僕僕地齊聚台北，為著下世代數位新潮流趨勢，進行為期四天的全球 ICT 政策發展專題會議。

　　對你我來說，這場四天的世界資訊科技大會（World Congress on Information Technology，簡稱 WCIT）或許無關緊要，但對全世界的資訊科技人來講，這好比是場科技業的「奧林匹克」盛會！尤其是這次 WCIT 大會邀請來的 9 位演講者，都是世界級的科技領袖，包括：

1. 世界經濟論壇資深總監 Alan Marcus
   從「數位時代根基」來看國家網路整體評比、資通訊服務的整合，及軟硬體創新探討國家競爭力。

2. MIT Lab 創辦人和主持人 Alex Sandy Pentland
   談論個人資料之巨量分析，如何促進政府服務與經濟。

3. 德國循環經濟龍頭科思創執行長 Patrick Thomas

4. Solar Impulse 創辦人 Bertrand Piccard

5. 前經濟部長李世光
   3、4、5，這三位共同探討循環經濟及永續發展的影響。

6. 日本電信電話公司社長岩本敏男（Toshio Iwamoto）
   談論資通訊科技發展之衍生與創新。

7. Azure 之父、微軟企業副總裁 Jason Zander
   分享物聯網如何改變世界。

8. 飛利浦照明全球戰略負責人 Bill Bien

    從明日城市發展所需之綠能與智慧科技，探討城市推動發展政策及趨勢。

9. 三菱電機前社長下村節宏（Setsuhiro Shimomura）

    分享數位工廠為何被視為工業 4.0 的基礎。

　　從這九位 V.I.P. 所分享資通訊創新趨勢及前瞻思維便可得知：WCIT 對於未來智慧生活方向有舉足輕重的影響。總統蔡英文、行政院院長賴清德、行政院政務委員吳政忠、政務委員唐鳳、國發會副主委曾旭正、經濟部部長沈榮津、台北市市長柯文哲等官員都出席開幕典禮及與會，尤其一連四天的數位夢想大展，是政府各部會以及各企業、法人單位首次跨域、跨界，一起同心協助台灣產業升級轉型！充分展現了台灣近年來在軟體創新與系統優異的整合能力，讓全世界都見識到台灣轉型「數位國家、智慧島嶼」的傲人成果！

　　是誰讓這場久違的科技盛會在台灣發生？又是誰讓全世界都清楚看見台灣從「資訊硬體代工大國」成功轉型為「資訊應用數位強國」的堅強實力？

　　幕後功臣究竟是誰？

這必須從 2016 年，邱月香女士上任世界資訊科技暨服務業聯盟（World Information Technology & Services Alliance, WITSA）主席一職開始說起：她是 WITSA 成立以來，第一位來自台灣的主席！更成功說服大會改變章程，使原本兩年一次舉辦的科技盛會，改為一年一次，也為台灣成功爭取主辦權。

　　2017 年，台灣成為第一個單年舉辦 WCIT 的國家！同年 12 月成立 WITSA 台北辦公室，上任後更馬不停蹄地拜訪各國政商鉅子、促進國際交流，參與聯合國經濟圓桌論壇，邱月香以「科技外交、整合行銷」成功地讓全世界看見台灣源源不絕的動力！

　　一個來自台灣的女子，如何從一個清苦的客家家庭，努力學習而後隻身前往美國闖蕩，終致躍上國際舞台、引領台灣串聯起全球頂尖的資訊科技──Soft power is changing the world──她傳奇的故事，且聽她娓娓道來。

創新、突破、開創新局，
為台灣創造新價值

宏碁集團創辦人／智榮基金會董事長　施振榮

中華民國資訊軟體協會成立於 1983 年，當時我剛當選台北市電腦公會（TCA）理事長，台灣 IT 產業也才剛開始發展。在我任內，我推動 TCA 由原本以內銷為主，改為以外銷為主的組織，由於 IT 產業的國際市場大，加上正值成長期，因此產業蓬勃發展。

相對之下，由於軟體協會以國內市場為主，當時軟體的國內市場較有限，加上觀念上一般又對硬體的重視程度大於軟體，因此配置在軟體的預算也相對有限，且國內最大客戶——政府又將資訊服務專案優先委任資策會，因此軟體產業發展較難以規模化，能創造的價值也受限。

直到近年在資訊應用普及之下，市場對軟體的需求提升，未來台灣軟體產業的發展如何借重硬體在國際上的基礎，進一步在上面加值以創造更多附加價值，將是重要的發展策略。

此外，推動軟體產業的發展策略也要有新的思維，要特別重視以內需來帶動外銷，台灣是各種資訊應用服務最佳的實驗場，我們可以在台灣先練兵，待做出成功的典範後，進一步拓展國際化的市場，透過 IT 的軟硬體整合在國際上更上一層樓。

邱理事長在本書中分享許多她的理念，與我所推動的理念也正好吻合，尤其她爭取擔任 WITSA（世界資訊科技暨服務業聯盟）主席，讓台灣在國際上的能見度提升，加上她的積極與創新思維，協助軟協轉型，開創新局。

在 2018 年 8 月，由中華軟協所主辦的「2018 資訊服務產業策略會議」，邀請宏碁集團創辦人、財團法人智榮文教基金會董事長施振榮演講，邱月香並致贈感謝函合影

軟協在今年 8 月 28 日舉辦資訊服務產業的策略會議，邱理事長特別與我討論策略會議的方向，同時也請我協助邀請部分講者。此次策略會議以推動產業的創新轉型為目的，配合政府推動「5+2+2」產業創新計畫，聚焦以「文化科技」與「智慧城鄉」為兩大主題，當天我也以「建設智慧城鄉 發揚東方矽文明」為題演講。

我認為這是具前瞻性且務實的策略方向，極具未來性，也是台灣資訊服務產業未來發展的重要方向。惟如要進一步有效落實，就有賴政府政策引導，藉由創造市場需求，讓台灣業界有將創新落實的舞台；其次在台灣練兵後，要進一步以國際為市場，讓台灣對國際社會做出更多貢獻。

相信軟協及 WITSA 在邱理事長帶領下，定能扮演關鍵的角色，而書中她也提出她對未來發展的願景，我也十分期待未來的發展，希望有朝一日能為台灣創造更多新的價值。

我眼中的邱月香——
展現包容力、真誠感染國內外人士

宏碁資訊服務股份有限公司　萬以寧董事長專訪

辦公室裡案頭上的公文如一座座小山，窗台處擺放著整齊的文房四寶，工整的書法如風簷展讀。來到宏碁位於台北的辦公室，拜訪宏碁資訊服務股份有限公司萬以寧董事長，同時身兼中華民國資訊軟體協會常務理事，身姿挺拔的萬以寧坐姿挺立，倒像是文人畫裡走出的名士。

● 真誠 & OUT OF BOX THINKING

對於邱理事長在中華軟協的成就，這位科技界老兵給予極高的評價：「中華軟協是一個真誠相處的組織，大家同舟共濟，希望在產業與國際上有所作為，有更突破性的發展。在台灣這個以硬體掛帥的環境中，邱理事長和其他人的背景都不一樣，那時我們想找一個 out of box thinking 的人，或許能打開不同的局面，但沒想到她的努力、認真和創新真的超乎想像。」

「她的真誠讓團隊有了溫度，像個大家庭。家，就是有話就講的地方，無論是對內部同事、對政府單位，或海外人士，都會被她的真誠感染。她對人的關心與細膩，不是一般人能及，她也展現很高的包容力，願意多方諮詢尋求意見。」

● 博采眾長，讓團隊變成一個家

宛若名士評點人物、青梅煮酒。

「書的智慧是活的：『三十輻，共一轂，當其無，有車之用。埏埏以為器，鑿戶牖以為室[1]。』這是老子的智慧，空的東西才能海納百川，也正因為她的心態開放，會聽取意見來調整大方向，讓一個團隊發揮集體智慧。中華軟協的素質很好，正直、紀律，而她在這個基礎上又做了突破。」

● 突破：展現氣度與統合力

提到「out of box thinking」，萬以寧立刻舉了一個最直接的例子：「2017 年，她打破傳統，推動第 21 屆世界資訊科技大會（WCIT）在台灣圓滿舉行！」

「理事長推展了國際平台，架構有了，創造創新等內容必須要跟上，前面闖出來的國際關係才能開花結果。發展智慧城市，推動 AI，這是大趨勢。台灣充滿創業精神，政府又大力支持，又有場域可以做實驗，加上台灣的 SI 公司是很強的，硬體、軟體、服務、創新等能力完全具備，中華軟協也有相關機制進行整合。這些能量未來要能跟著理事長領導中華軟協創造出來的國際平台走出去，那就是真正的發揮台灣的 Soft Power 了。」盱衡局勢，萬以寧爽朗的笑聲，為整個台灣資訊科技的宏觀願景，下了一個最好的註解！

---

[1] 三十輻，共一轂，當其無，有車之用。埏埴以為器，當其無，有器之用。鑿戶牖以為室，當其無，有室之用。故有之以為利，無之以為用。～《老子道德經‧第十一章》意思是：三十條車輻彙集到一根轂的孔洞當中，有了車轂中空的地方把木頭合在一起，車子才可以發揮作用載人。揉和陶土做成器皿，有了中空的地方，才有器皿的作用。開鑿門窗建造房屋，房子裡面有了空間，才有房屋的功用。所以，有給人的便利，是因為「無」發揮了它的作用。

我認識的邱月香——
跳脫框架的首位女性中華軟協理事長

巨匠電腦　鍾梁權董事長專訪

　　巨匠，台灣電腦教育的龍頭，三十多年來為台灣孕育了無數電腦專才。創辦人鍾梁權董事長，同時也是中華民國資訊軟體協會常務理事，一路上看著台灣軟體業的發展。我們來到巨匠座落於台北市公園路的總部，一訪這位電腦教育界的巨擘。

● 多元化的首位女性理事長

　　宏亮的聲音、親切的笑容，帶著幾分豪俠的爽朗是鍾梁權給人的第一印象。

　　鍾梁權爽朗地說：「我在中華軟協二十二年，邱理事長是中華軟協第一位女性理事長，上任後，她更是全心全職的投入。」果然是大俠，一語破的：「成立三十幾年的中華軟協，她是第七位理事長，我與她認識十六、七年，她曾擔任中華民國電腦學會的副理事長，她的才華橫溢、毅力驚人，因為她這樣的特質，我們邀請她加入中華軟協。早期軟體產業是以工程師背景、男性為主的專業導向，她雖然不是工程師出身，但她涉獵範圍廣泛，兼具軟性、理性與感性、融入多元化的特性，為協會注入非典型的另類活力。」

● 海納百川：將中華軟協從國家帶領到國際

　　說到激昂處，鍾梁權的手飛舞了起來，彷如豪俠展演招式；「她帶領協會邁入第五年，讓整個產業的感覺變得非常不一樣，擁有不同的樣貌，更因為她與人為善的特質，不分藍綠都支持她，上至總統、部長，整個建立良好的關係，這是歷任理事長中做的最淋漓盡致的一任！更因為擔任 WITSA 主席，將中華軟協從台灣帶領到全世界，她本人的熱衷、本身的特性、語文能力好又喜歡與人為善，讓協會在國際上的能見度有了更多的突破。」對於邱月香的事蹟，鍾梁權如數家珍的說：「她的度量與包容心很大，就算與我們意見不合也會採納，正是這種海納百川有容乃大的特性，讓她將這份職務發揚光大。」

● 紮根：吸引人才

針對「多元化」，鍾梁權提到了邱月香「資訊一定要往下紮根」的堅持：「以前協會較專注在軟體產業上的發展，理事長上任後開始進入學校，辦理講座，讓大專院校的學生更了解中華軟協，向下紮根吸引人才進入軟體業。未來才能為國家帶入更多元的新血與活力，她人格的特質，讓一切變得非常自然，這些都不是以獲利承接業務為前題，是純粹先以『服務』為導向，讓協會的多元性更提高，這是一個很大的突破跟改變。」

● 跌倒再站起來，展現無比毅力

「中華軟協理事長是選舉制的，但從監事要選理事長在協會的慣例是跳躍式的，她願意跳出來為大家服務，展現無比的企圖心及毅力。」鍾梁權更舉了一件往事，說明邱月香無人能比的驚人毅力：「在競選理事長的過程中，因一次運動意外跌倒，她的髖關節破裂，要動手術，但她希望，在她上任的第一天主持會議，不用任何輔助！試想：女性髖關節破裂那是多麼大的事！一般人起碼恢復期也要六個月，但她兩個月就行動自如！」鍾梁權露出讚嘆的神情：「從這個地方可以看到她的毅力驚人！只要設定目標，就一定去完成。一般人可能因為這個變故，就退出了，但她還是堅持到底。這正是為什麼她能當選中華軟協理事長暨 WITSA 主席的最佳寫照。」

訪談中鍾梁權沒有重複的字句，唯獨「非常」這兩字重複了兩次，也正因為邱月香有著「非常」之毅力，才能有「非常」之成就。她以 WITSA 主席的影響力在聯合國發聲，在國際軟體界扮演關鍵的角色，帶領著中華民國資訊軟體協會在國際上不論是關係、人脈或是舞台都更形寬廣，而 WITSA 主席的角色，更是突破區域的限制，讓影響更加深遠。

我所認識的邱月香——
不斷為台灣出力奔波的軟協理事長

　　認識邱月香是在我待了近 30 年的一個社會團體——九陽會，那時候她剛剛當選中華民國軟體協會的理事長，只感覺她精力充沛，對於人、事、物特別有溫度，只知道她公司本業是從事電腦教育的工作，對於資訊教育不遺餘力，也頗具愛心，出錢出力幫助台灣的包括中小學及大專院校年輕人出國參加競賽，還獲得很不錯的世界競賽優異排名成績。同時還聽說協助台灣一些對於資訊安全的年輕人，端正學習方向，出錢出力協助他們創業並送他們出國參加國際競賽，免於淪入不法駭客之途，洋溢著邱媽媽母雞的長者風範。

　　幾年前在一次高爾夫運動的球賽中，她不幸跌倒，髖關節給摔裂了，住院手術治療後，我卻常常在九陽會例會以及中華軟協其他資訊活動中，看到她忍著傷痛、拄著拐杖出席活動，為朋友情誼以及台灣資訊工業產業盡力，毅力著實令人感動！更令人吃驚的是她憑著一股使命感以及毅力，在不被看好的氛圍下，忍著傷痛越洋參加世界級的 WITSA 墨西哥世界資訊年會，競選 WITSA 主席並當選，相信這是台灣在世界資訊工業史上的第一人，同時還成功爭取到擁有全球 83 個國家會員的 WITSA 資訊年會 WCIT 於 2017 年在台灣舉辦，相距上一次 WCIT 2000 年在台舉辦的時間，整整相距 17 年，這讓世界各國都看傻了眼，也欽佩台灣這位奇女子的能耐！ 2017 年 WCIT 年會在台灣結合政府以及民間的努力獲得成功的事實，也不禁讓我對她的公關、組織、協調以及毅力大為佩服！

現今國際現實，台灣在國際上不斷地被打壓，壓縮我們國際上的空間，但是邱月香卻能夠以 WITSA 國際主席的身分，突破困境在國際上穿梭，不論是在聯合國殿堂上或是和我們台灣沒有邦交的一些國家，她都能輕易見到總理、總統或是資訊工業相關重要閣員，為台灣發聲宣傳，以民間城市對城市、公協會對公協會的實質關係，替台灣產業奔波。這位國際級的理事長目前仍馬不停蹄地造訪世界各國，結合台灣國內產業，以她所創造出來的國際平台，為台灣產業的未來不斷尋找出路，這種毅力以及使命感，著實令人感佩！

Ms. Chiu's exemplary leadership, and countless achievements

亞美尼亞Ucom, IUnetworks **聯合創辦人***Alexandr Yesayan*

It has been an absolute honor for me to work closely with Ms. Chiu over the past years on the organization of the World Congress on Information Technology (WCIT), taking place in Yerevan, Armenia in October 2019. Ms. Chiu's vision, experience, and abundant support have played and continue to play a crucial role in surpassing each milestone leading up to the event.

As the 1st female Chairperson of WITSA, Ms. Chiu's exemplary leadership, and countless achievements have been the embodiment of women empowerment. Her strength and resilience in the face of challenges, in addition to her remarkable problem-solving ability in a swift, efficient, and diplomatic manner have been invaluable assets for us, in particular whilst requesting the support of different stakeholders to ensure the success of WCIT in Armenia.

As I write this introduction, Ms. Chiu has visited Yerevan on three separate occasions. Given her hectic schedule, this alone serves as proof of her relentless dedication to every project she's involved in.

I look forward to celebrating Ms. Chiu's many more successes to come.

Yvonne Chiu, Santiago Gutierrez Testimonial

Santiago Gutierrez, Chairman Emeritus, WITSA

I met Yvonne in the turmoil of the WCIT 2014 in Guadalajara, Mexico. She arrived directly from her twenty something hours flight straight to the conferenceroom where the WITSA Board was holding its meeting. She dressed like a company top notch executive and that was a good start for a first impression.

During the meeting, that good impression was confirmed through her interventions and participation in the meeting. She had not met yet most of the Board Directors and suddenly she came forward with an unexpected proposal: she offered to undertake the WCIT 2017 in Taipei City. It was more surprising due to the fact that Taiwan had already celebrated WCIT 2000 in Taipei as well.

That was the beginning of a fruitful career in WITSA and of our friendship.

I would like to congratulate Ms Chiu on becoming WITSA's 1st female Chairman. Her dedication to the spirit of WITSA's vision of *Fulfilling the Promise of the Digital Age*, where everyone, regarding of who they or where they reside receives the benefits of Information and Communication Technology. As the former chairman of WITSA representing the country of Mexico for four years, I know well what effort it took to be selected as WITSA's chairman considering the diversity of cultures and the levels of development WITSA members represent.

The dedication to WITSA that Ms Chiu has demonstrated in the period of time she has held the office of WITSA Chairman (2016-2018) is remarkable. She has unselfishly given her time and energy to work with WITSA members in scores of counties around the globe. It is a very good feeling to know that when I completed my term as chairman a very qualified successor not only stepped in to continue the good work of WITSA but excelled as its chairman.

目　錄

第一章 初見

出席聯合國會議的科技女董座

第二章 「香」自苦寒來

貧困淬礪出的超級女「客」

第三章 翻轉教育

全額資助清貧孩子出國摘金

第四章 資安教母
不計心力推動資安立法

第五章 活躍社交與溫柔心靈

第六章　WITSA 主席之路
從 CISA 到 WITSA 鏈結台灣與世界

第七章　鳳凰展翅
前進聯合國

初見

出席聯合國會議的
科技女董座

WITSA 台北辦公室

　　2017 年 12 月 WITSA 台北辦公室於內湖瑞光路成立，向外遠眺半個台北盡收眼底，WITSA 世界資訊科技暨服務業聯盟，由 83[2] 個國家的資訊與通訊同業團體組成，參與會議的人士來自各國政府、企業、學術、非營利組織等科技領導者。而這個全球最大的資通訊服務產業組織主席——邱月香女士——來自台灣，同時也是中華民國資訊軟體協會[3]（CISA）的理事長。

　　一個來自台灣的女性是如何登上國際性組織的主席？在現今的國際情勢下，又是如何披荊斬棘，一路走來突破艱辛的外交困境？想到這裡，更讓人好奇是怎樣的堅持與信念，以台灣的資訊科技掙出了聯合國裡的一席之地！

---

[2] 有「全世界最快樂的國家」之稱的不丹，在邱月香前往拜訪，並當面的邀請下，已於 2018 年 8 月 22 日成為第 83 個會員國。

[3] 中華民國資訊軟體協會，英文名稱為 Information Service Industry Association of R.O.C.，簡稱 CISA。

初次接觸

在 WITSA 台北會議室裡，看著遠方的 101 大樓，第一次來這裡，是去年 12 月 WITSA 台北辦公室的成立記者會，當時現場來了多國代表，可謂冠蓋雲集儼然一個聯合國聚會。

穿過辦公區，來到了主席辦公室，素雅的裝潢間或綴著雅緻的擺設，幾件小物不經意透露出主人的童心。眼前只見一位雍容典雅的女士優雅的坐在沙發上，胸前繽紛深邃的珍珠項鍊襯著淡粉色的妝容，大器中又多了幾分親近。

「坐吧！」清亮的嗓音伴著月彎似的笑容，眼前這位有如多寶格裡珍藏的玲瓏仕女，她，就是：「世界資訊科技暨服務業聯盟」WITSA 的主席──邱月香。

紳士學院 ── 老闆們的電腦教室

　　90 年代邱月香自美國回台，發現台灣很多人連開機都不會，一心想為台灣做事的她深深地明白，未來是電腦的時代，國外的科技正以一日千里的飛速前進，要讓台灣跟上世界的潮流刻不容緩。而「紳士學院」便在此機緣下由邱月香一手創生。

　　正因為在國外的歷練，讓邱月香對台灣更憂心也更見真情；「當時有很多台灣的中小企業老闆們連開機都不會，我告訴他們：『現在不會使用電腦，將來就是文盲』！」因為這樣「取之於社會，用之於社會」的誠意，讓當時的台北縣長蘇貞昌都讚歎她是「尚水ㄟ校長」！

　　隨著提升電腦教育的紳士學院展開，久經商場的老闆們再次回到了學校，紳士學院更成了老闆們彼此交流學習的平台。

推廣電腦教育引起中華軟協注意

　　當年為中華民國電腦教育發展協會副理事長的邱月香，為了幫助補教業者在「人才培訓案」，向政府單位爭取合理權益，並且要求「公平公正公開」的政府公聽會，優異的居中斡旋能力，引起了中華民國資訊軟體協會的注意，在中華軟協理監事的極力邀請下，邱月香進入中華軟協，並擔任了12年的理監事。

　　在中華軟協深耕了12年，協會的人都叫邱月香一聲大姊，這聲「大姊」背後包含了多少的付出！在中華軟協22年、台灣電腦教育界龍頭——巨匠電腦鐘梁權董事長便說道：「當時因為人才培訓案讓很多會員向協會尋求協助，協會成員裡很多是承接政府的委辦單位，但政府採購的要求高、毛利低，很多成員都吃不消，有的虧損甚至倒閉。邱月香進入中華軟協後透過她的人脈，帶動會員業務上的拓展。」

　　正因為她在國外的歷練，看到了不同的面向，引進全新的策略方針，進入中華軟協後更提出了會員專屬服務，及參與多項公益活動，讓會員在中華軟協裡有了截然不同的附加意義！效率之快更讓人耳目一新，這一路行來，是怎樣的披荊斬棘造就了她，更將她推進了聯合國？邱月香的「柔、軟」奮鬥，現在才要開始！

「香」自苦寒來

貧困淬礪出的超級女「客」

客家背景：慈母嚴父

「小時候台北市中正路上 1616 號的『金魚理髮院』，就是我生長的地方，爸爸從龍潭踩著三輪車載著媽媽上台北打拼。家裡還未發達的時候，常需要借錢周轉，因為家裡開理髮院，從小就需要幫忙洗頭洗毛巾。」看著邱月香悠遠的眼神，跟著回到了那個台灣經濟起飛，人們誠懇勤奮的年代。

「看到家裡的清苦，拿到的獎學金、薪水都會先給媽媽。我媽媽沒有讀過書，連 ABC 都不會，可是她很堅持要我學英文，當時我也不懂她為什麼那麼固執。」

邱月香嘴角微微上揚：「年輕時不懂為什麼要學英文，每次媽媽問起學得如何，我都用 How are you、Fine、Thank you 帶過。」主席優雅的臉龐漾開了一抹微笑，彷彿回到當年呼攏媽媽的淘氣女孩。

「我爸爸很嚴；」說到這段兒時往事，邱月香還是有點不開心：「只要有男生打電話來，他都說『邱月香不在！』明明我就坐在旁邊耶！也不能去游泳，露營更不用說了！」但其實邱月香心裡明白：「父親是愛之深，責之切。」

她憶起父親童年時的要求：「小時候爸爸要我們一定要學會客家話，強調母語的重要性。即使那是個學校只能講國語不能說其他方言的年代。我爸爸是個不會就要學到會的人，他甚至半開玩笑地警告我

邱月香全家福

們：『如果哪天要在阿爸牌位前求事情，如果不用客家話來跟阿爸講，阿爸是絕對不會理你們的喔！』阿爸也曾再三告誡我們：『一定要當個先知先覺的人。如果能力不夠好，也要先知後覺、或後知先覺，絕不能當個不知不覺的人！』」

回首前塵 —— 理髮院裡的辛酸往事

上有兩個哥哥、下有三個弟弟，每次開學的時候都還得借錢才能念書。「念商職的時候，有時事情沒做完就要趕去上課，那時心裡很難過……」時光流轉，小小的月香依然在理髮院裡忙活著 —— 休學，成了她對家的成全。回憶伴著哽咽。在理髮院裡，親戚朋友的孩子來學技術，做錯了事，媽媽只是說說而已，對自己卻是大聲責罵。水龍頭的水嘩啦啦地流著，她的淚往心裡淌著。小小的月香不明白，「我是妳女兒妳怎麼對別人比較好」。很多年以後，月香才懂當時母親的苦心。

邱月香自小和媽媽感情甚篤，在美國德州工作時亦邀請媽媽一同出遊

● 善導寺師父的一句話助她重返校園

一天，店門被推開了，月香眼前一亮，只見善導寺的師父走了進來，說要剃頭。月香像往常一樣地在店裡忙著，「妹妹這麼乖，怎麼都在幫忙！要去念念書啊！」師父開了口對爸爸說道。

「到了開學那一天，爸爸竟真的讓我去念書！」從沉沉的回憶裡抽回，「再回到學校，我就很認真，都拿獎學金。」邱月香笑了笑，「後來我爸爸靠著自學轉入房地產業後，經營有成，家中經濟變好了，現在某些著名建商，當時都會來向爸爸請益。」

或許正是這樣深深刻印在骨子裡的客家精神造就了她，休學後復學，更加珍惜這得來不易的機會！

而她一口流利的英語，卻是靠她跟她口中的「外國爸媽」自學而來的！

西方文化的衝擊與洗禮

　　原來，邱月香在就讀淡水工商管理專科學校（現真理大學）時，開始在外國家庭教小朋友中文。爸爸叫 Roy Hall，是美軍顧問團的律師，媽媽是 Joyce。全家都是很虔誠的教徒，為了更瞭解美國的文化，週末邱月香也跟著一起上教堂。在那裡，她學會了西餐禮儀，並和他們培養起像家人一樣的深厚感情。「我還特地去買刀叉回家練習，我媽看了還罵我：『妳起肖！』」邱月香不自覺地笑了起來，「後來還到教堂受洗，當時只覺得受洗水好冷。記得當時外國爸爸說：『Good for you』，我只是想洗一洗比較乾淨，但我心裡明白：上帝是勸人為善的。其實西方很鼓勵發問，英文不懂我就去問，還會寫英文文章請外國爸爸修改。」

　　訪談中邱月香不時微笑，國台英語自然交會，也難怪她自由穿梭在本土與國際之間游刃有餘，正因為她年少時經歷不同的文化交融。

　　隨著中美斷交，Roy 要帶著全家回美國。當年台灣尚未如今日消息通達，全國上下都很擔心沒有美國這個盟友，台灣的未來何去何從。邱月香也很害怕地問外國爸爸 Roy：「台灣，會有問題嗎？」

　　沒想到，Roy 卻是氣定神閒地回答她：「妳放心好了，台灣的戰略地位，很、重、要！」

　　當時的邱月香只把這句話當成安慰，涉世未深的她並不知道 Roy 的深謀遠慮。時至今日，她回想起當年 Roy 的胸有成竹，不禁嘆道：

邱月香與外國爸媽：Roy Hall 和 Joyce 全家合影

「外國爸爸在四十年前，就已經知道台灣戰略地位的重要性了。」

　　後來他們回去了阿拉巴馬州。「我後來還曾到美國找他們敘舊呢。」但此刻邱月香原本高昂的嗓音逐漸轉為低沉：「沒想到第二次再相見的原因，竟是媽媽 Joyce 打電話，告訴我外國爸爸去世了……我到阿拉巴馬，在他的墳前獻花。回想起當年在他們身上學到的無私及關心，真的很感念他們一家人。」

在台經營貿易公司，開啟出國契機

60 年代月香家的理髮院旁開著一家大同醫院，總是在店裡忙碌著的月香看著鄰居一家常常出國，小小的心靈裡也鼓勵自己：「總有一天我也要出去看看！」

1976 年，二十出頭的她便隻身前往美國闖蕩。早在出國前，邱月香在台灣已成立貿易公司，因為貿易的往來常出國拜訪客戶，認識了很多外國友人，富於觀察與好奇的她也因此學到很多的異國文化。曾有一位奧克拉荷馬州的老先生來台灣吃西餐時總是喝著 007 龐德的最愛——馬丁尼，這綴著綠橄欖的馬丁尼引起了她的注意，經過多次觀察，年輕的邱月香忍不住問：「為什麼你只喝馬丁尼？」老先生回答：「因為上流社會的紳士們都是這麼喝的啊！」從此以後，High Class 的馬丁尼成了邱月香的佐餐酒，她笑著說：「從小我就是這樣：只要我在別人身上看到值得學習、模仿的地方，我都會牢牢記住，讓自己更快融入異國的文化及禮儀。」

台美往來之間認識了西北航空的 captain 與他的家人，每當邱月香前往西雅圖，captain 便會安排聚會，邱月香因此認識了更多的外國友人，正因為這些好朋友開啟了她前往美國闖蕩的契機。

初生之犢不畏虎，單槍匹馬闖美國

「我先在西雅圖住了 8 年，70 年代的美國很少人認識台灣人，在朋友的介紹下，一個接一個，我認識了更多朋友。」邱月香笑了起來，哼起了歌謠：「透早就出門，天色漸漸光，受苦無人問……」，或許是鄉愁，隻身在異國的她，每天出門都會哼著這鄉土小調為自己加油。

一個年輕的異國女孩就這樣在美國開疆闢土，初到異國的她凡事勤儉，但做傢俱生意需要包裝紙材，一份就要美金 5 元！這時一位朋友告訴她：*The Seattle Times*（《西雅圖時報》）他們印報剩下的紙材可以拿去利用；另一個朋友告訴她，可以去賣文具的地方拿紙箱。就這樣，邱月香買了一輛廂型車，在朋友的幫忙與指引下，開始了她的生意。

當然，個頭嬌小、外型亮眼的邱月香也遇到不少有趣的事，例如剛到西雅圖的她去用餐，結帳時卻被告知已有人先行買單，她才發現「好像身邊有不少愛慕者」。又因為長相太過年輕，點酒時都會被檢查是否成年。剛開始她還得意地揚了揚身分證，告訴店家：「我的年紀可以喝酒了啦！」但每次去消費都被檢查也讓她不堪其擾。直到十多年後，她重返西雅圖，再到這間餐館用餐：「這一次呢……他們就沒有再來檢查我的年齡啦，虧我還早早就將身分證準備好呢，看來，這些年我也成熟不少了喔。」

「我那時頭髮是長的，別人問我，妳們家有幾個人，我不敢說只有我一個人，所以我都回答我們家有雙胞胎，長頭髮談生意的是Yvonne（邱月香的英文名），頭髮綁起來在做事的是Yvonny。」邱月香笑了起來：「沒想到所有客戶都信以為真，以為我有個雙胞胎姐妹，到後來竟沒有一個人發現不對勁！當時很多朋友說德州市場更大，聽完後我先在德州待一個禮拜，發現生意真的更廣闊，也開始在事前跟一些公司接洽談代理。」

到了德州，邱月香才發現以往對美國的認知是：進步、文明、還有時髦，但當地完全不是那麼一回事。她回憶起當年她走在德州鄉下，被路人指指點點的趣事：「美國鄉下完全沒見過東方人，尤其是像我這樣濃妝豔抹的東方女人。我問朋友這些路人為什麼一直指著我竊竊私語？我朋友笑著回答：『因為這些德州人以為妳是外星人！』」

臨危不亂 —— 拒絕墨西哥毒梟

　　一個人在美國打拚的邱月香，十分重視自身的安全。她養成許多保護自己的好習慣：例如她絕不跟客戶吃晚餐；在 Motel 住宿，她一定住在離櫃台最近的客房，就算有了危險還可以高聲呼救；太陽下山前一定要進到房間，沒到隔天日出絕不出門，也因此練就一身美甲好技術；用餐時只要離開座位，回來後就不再碰桌上的任何水杯；但無論她再怎麼小心，還是不能「未卜先知」。

　　有一回，邱月香和傢俱工廠的墨西哥老闆相約談代理。謹慎行事的她，請長年居住在洛杉磯的大專同學開車送她過去。而這次代理談的出乎意料地順利；「妳還沒吃飯吧！我請妳吃午餐。」正值中午，一路趕忙的 Yvonne 也確實餓了，心想這個墨西哥人真豪氣，不但什麼都答應，還要請我吃飯。

　　吃完了午餐，車子不是開回工廠，卻停在一棟豪宅中。ㄇ字型的兩層樓房，十幾部豪華轎車一字排開，樓上豪華的房間更多如飯店一般：各種不同的水晶燈映射著種種夢幻，每一個房間裡有著各自不同的風格，珍奇擺設，水晶映著炫目與驚奇！有如電影般的場景就在她眼前！「妳可以住在這裡。」墨西哥毒梟看著她：「要去哪兒，車子隨妳挑、隨妳開！」這下子強喝馬丁尼的 Yvonne，可真要成為龐德女郎了！

　　回到了墨西哥老闆的辦公室，老闆的電話響了，隱約之間，她不時聽到「powder」在對話裡流出，Yvonne 瞬間驚覺——「該不會⋯⋯這個老闆賣傢俱也賣毒品？！他在傢俱裡都藏毒！」該走？該逃？各種可能在她心裡來回上演，強忍著內心的不安，邱月香告訴自己千萬要鎮靜，也提高了警覺！

80 年代可不像現在大家都有手機，邱月香靈機一動，假借要與朋友聯絡的名義，借了電話向事先已知會的大專好姊妹求救，她同學立刻前來，邱月香連再見都不說，車子一到，兩人立馬狂飆離開。

這有如電影 007 一樣驚險的場景，面對誘惑而不心動，也只有比龐德女郎還令人驚豔的 Yvonne 能辦到了。

異國 Twin sister Linda Reisman

　　緩了緩語氣，邱月香回到了平時的淡定：「後來我到了德州，住在丹佛的 Linda Reisman 很照顧我，她看我一個小女生到丹佛做生意，就邀請我住在她家，還把她的車給我用。她的爸爸是美國猶太人，她都說我是她的 twin sister，還開玩笑說是她爸爸來美國時不小心把我從飛機上丟下去。」一掃剛才的緊張氛圍，爽朗如銀鈴般的笑聲充滿著房間：「我和她全家人的感情有如一家人一樣親密，她很會做菜，我也拿出我的絕活：做春捲、水餃分享給他們，並且宣揚台灣的『美食文化』。」

邱月香與 Linda Reisman 全家合影

闖蕩德州，事業有成

「在德州代理傢俱，賺到了錢就買了一輛賓士 500 來犒賞自己！還特別挑了一台綠色的！那時行動電話剛出來，我揹著黑金剛、穿著貂皮大衣，自己在洗車場洗車。我其實很自豪，因為這些都是我靠自己賺來的！」

為什麼會這麼說，因為她的確有「自傲」的本事！有一回她接到一個耶誕節前出貨的大訂單，但公司的訂單「規定」只能接到 10 月底，因為接下來的時間工廠要趕工，才能如期交貨。換言之，這張訂單就算送到老闆面前也無法出貨。邱月香心中雖急，但仍然苦思解決之道！轉念一想，就在傳真回公司的訂單上寫下大大的「Lush」四個英文字！沒多久，老闆的電話就來了！

「Lush 是什麼意思？」老闆焦急地問。

「我就在等這一通電話！」邱月香笑著解答：「我知道如果我寫正確的『rush』（急件），所有的業務也都會這樣寫，老闆可能不以為意，但如果我寫的是『Lush』，那他一定會因為好奇而打電話來詢問，我也『正好』請他務必幫忙，讓訂單如期出貨。」

就是這種「企圖心有多少，方法就有多少」的不服輸個性，邱月香在美創業，搖身成為事業有成的實業家，為自己累積了不一樣的身價。正是因為「天不怕地不怕」這樣的性格與經歷，形塑她超然的特質：生於客家、融合於美國，孕育出她獨一無二的 Soft power！邱月香說自己只知道要勇往直前，「在國外的時候，我都很樂觀地在過日子，因為——我沒有悲觀的權利！」

翻轉教育

全額資助清貧孩子
出國摘金

懷抱初心，回饋鄉里

所處的環境、身旁的氛圍，弱勢的孩子在原生環境裡是很難翻身的！是什麼樣的初心，讓嬌小的邱月香充滿動力，連年自掏腰包帶孩子們出國比賽呢？

「在美國時我曾經多次回台灣，每次回來都覺得台灣好溫暖。」邱月香雙手交握、平放胸前，緩緩倒向沙發：「每當想家的時候就開始唱《黃昏的故鄉》……」微閉著雙眼哼不到兩句，歌聲中記憶揉雜著思念，哽咽伴著鼻音：「我想起爸爸曾經再三叮囑，賺了錢就要回饋鄉里。」

90 年代初，旅美十餘年的成功女企業家回到了自己的故鄉，卻也開始了她另一段璀璨的資訊人生！

● 賀伯颱風募款音樂會

1996 年強烈颱風賀伯襲台，對全台灣造成嚴重影響，台北縣市多處嚴重淹水，全台經濟損失更超過新台幣 300 億！邱月香當時身為汐止教育會理事長，為了盡速重建災後學校，她四處奔走，邀請音樂家簡文秀、日本旅台名鋼琴家藤田梓與聲樂家呂麗莉舉辦募款音樂會，並將門票所得，及來自資策會的 50 台電腦一併捐助給汐止有需要的學校。邱月香謙虛地說自己的登高一呼只是拋磚引玉，但也喚起社會大眾對救災與教育的共襄盛舉。

邱月香為汐止受災學校舉辦募款音樂會（左為聲樂家
簡文秀）

從地方到中央：舉辦全國電腦繪圖比賽

隨著汐止的學校重建推動，正好更新電腦設備。「想起在美國的時候，看到了電腦科技的進步，我發現，這正是台灣所需要的！那時心中立即升起一個念頭——要給這些弱勢的孩子一個翻身機會，而電腦人才正是台灣所欠缺的，何不教育這些孩子，讓他們有一技之長，為孩子們開一扇窗，又能為台灣培育人才！」當年，正是電腦升級 486 的年代：「我與當時的汐止鎮鎮長周雅淑、教育部電子計算機中心副主任劉金和，以及『草莓軟體[4]』 大家一同通力合作，每週六舉辦兒童電腦繪圖比賽，這在當時可是全國首創，就連教育部也都嘖嘖稱奇。」

「為了讓孩子們有學習動力，我創造一個良性的競爭環境，孩子們有了成就感，就會自發性的學習。學習的人多了，電腦風氣自然就帶了起來。」

---

[4] 草莓軟體 BerrySoft 於 1992 年 7 月成立，於 2000 年 4 月正名為草莓資訊有限公司，草莓軟體根據不同學齡階段，推出多樣化的輔助學習教材，讓小學生、家長及教師在數位工具的輔助下學習電腦課程。

為帶動台灣電腦風氣，邱月香在汐止舉辦青少年電腦繪圖比賽

國際接軌：強化電腦教育

　　說到這些孩子的表現，邱月香的臉上洋溢著自傲光彩！「我先將台灣的資訊紮根，把台灣的孩子基礎建立好，跟國際水平並駕齊驅，就能站上國際的舞台！讓台灣孩子的電腦實力可以跟國際接軌！」她深信：「弭平數位落差，就要從台灣的每一個角落開始做起！」

　　帶著母性的慈愛、更有著企業家的豪情：「我給孩子們一個舞台，讓他們有機會表現自己！從地區的競爭，拉到國際的競爭，讓大家有一個向心力，我對他們說：『只要你們努力，一定可以拿到國際大獎！』」從電腦的師資培育開始，逐步地規劃，邱月香從汐止鎮出發，將台灣的孩子推向世界舞台！

● MOS 世界盃電腦應用技能競賽

　　21 世紀初，邱月香恰巧遇到了美國友人，當時微軟正推展 Office 專業認證，深耕電腦教育多年的她，發現正和她對國際趨勢的觀察不謀而合，遂成立翊利得資訊科技有限公司取得 Microsoft Office 國際電腦專業認證台灣總代理——MOS，是 Microsoft Office Specialist 的縮寫，中文稱之為「Microsoft Office 專家認證」，是唯一獲得微軟認可的國際性 Office 軟體專業認證，翻譯成 27 種語言，通用全球 153 個國家地區。邱月香親自拜訪國內多所高中職、大專院校及補教機構，輔導學生考證，讓台灣的孩子一證在手，便可成為通行世界的國際人才！

2000 年，第一次參加世界盃電腦應用技能競賽出國比賽，邱月香與選手們跟呂秀蓮副總統（左二）合影

　　為了推展台灣、接軌國際，每年 5 月邱月香都會舉辦台灣的全國競賽，再由其中表現優異者組隊出國比賽。2008 年，第八年舉辦的 MOS 世界盃電腦應用技能競賽，首度分北、中、南三區競賽。當年，創辦台灣 MOS 證照考試的邱月香頒獎致詞時表示：「弭平數位落差，必須從台灣的每一個角落、每一個孩子開始做起！」這些競賽的真正目的，是要讓台灣的孩子能夠在電腦技能上與國際接軌，在國際競賽時，能夠和世界各國的冠軍進行交流，進而成為朋友，拓展國際視野。她要當台灣的比爾蓋茲，也希望參加比賽的學生能成為日後台灣的比爾蓋茲！

17 年來，邱月香為了幫台灣培育國際資訊人才，協助超過 70 多萬名學生取得國際相關證照。當初因緣際會走入資訊領域，進而推動資訊教育的她，面對世界即將洶湧而至的科技狂潮，非科班出身的邱月香明白，這 17 年來的心血，一定能內化為台灣未來資訊產業更雄厚的實力，帶領著台灣邁向更廣闊的世界。

● 全額資助清貧孩子

　　正因為年幼讀書時，繳學費還得跟親戚借錢的感受深深烙印在心裡，邱月香對清寒的孩子更是有如母親般的疼惜，並幫助無數清貧孩子取得國際專業證照：「清寒不用證明，只要老師、教授推薦即可。」她體貼又心疼地說道：「做公益是好事，但千萬不要造成孩子們二次傷害。」

2008 年，由於參賽選手眾多，台灣首次舉辦北中南三區競賽，足見邱月香推廣的電腦教育遍及全國各地

連續七年，共獲九座世界冠軍

　　2008 年以前，當時的世界盃電腦應用技能競賽只有 Word、Excel 等的比賽，但常與國際交流的邱月香早已察覺世界趨勢，提出自己的想法。

　　「我跟主辦單位說：現在每個人都需要 presentation，不只在學校報告，未來在社會上面試、介紹產品、建議提案都需要。這是兼顧重要且實用的技能，你們應該要舉辦 PowerPoint 的比賽。」

　　2009 年，來自全球 53 個國家、8 萬多名選手，參賽人數是開辦以來最多的一年，經歷了當地、國家、地區的各輪競賽，台灣爭取最後進入加拿大多倫多總冠軍決賽的資格！那一年，台灣終於贏得第一個世界冠軍！那一天，邱月香流下了眼淚，所有的付出化成了甜美的果實，報章媒體爭相報導這載譽歸國的台灣之光。接著，連續七年，邱月香親手培育的孩子們，為台灣奪得了九座世界冠軍！

2009 年，台灣首次在世界盃電腦應用技能競賽中奪得世界冠軍！

We are from Taiwan. Not China!

隔年邱月香再次領軍在美國猶他州比賽，台灣學生再度蟬連世界第一，勇奪兩座世界雙料冠軍！但就在中午頒獎時，司儀卻將得獎隊伍「From Taiwan」唸成「From China」，邱月香當下就拍桌抗議：「We are from Taiwan. Not China!」並要求對方連說三次「From Taiwan」以正視聽，理直氣壯的她把一旁的州長都給嚇了一大跳！

到了晚上頒獎前，邱月香提早到了大會。國際認證機構的夥伴跑來對邱月香說：「Yvonne, what can I do?」這沒來由的一句，邱月香疑惑地反問：「What?」

原來是有人要求將台灣的國旗換成中華台北，當時邱月香與對方的生意高達 100 萬美金，率真的她霸氣回應：「Do you want my business or not?」機構的夥伴急了：「I want Your business, but I don't know what to do. They change your flag, tell me what to do!」

當時各國的國旗是用電腦螢幕在會場呈現，已經刪除掉的中華民國國旗檔案無法救回；「Give me a few seconds!」邱月香爭取到時間，苦思該如何處理，忽然間，靈光一閃，她立刻提出她的解決之道！

「Delete all the flags and don't show!」

有如天降甘霖般，合作機構的夥伴也覺得這是最棒的解決辦法！「That I can do.」幾秒的時間內，邱月香做了最棒並且能做到的雙贏決策！並反制了國際上的打壓，敲出漂亮的一記全壘打。

愈慈悲心裡愈平靜

「烏拉圭的總統是最窮的總統,他說過:『愈慈悲心裡愈平靜。』」當談到這十餘年自費帶清貧孩子出國摘金,邱月香微笑說:「能讓台灣孩子跟世界第一流選手一較長短,在國際上揚眉吐氣,還有什麼比這些成果更值得的呢?」

● 外交官跟著孩子一起叫「邱媽」

為了讓台灣的孩子出國比賽不會失態,邱月香幫他們提早接觸國際禮儀和練習英文:「畢竟我們每一次的出征都是代表台灣!」為了讓孩子們無後顧之憂,她開始向外交部爭取補助,一個孩子一萬塊!巧的是每次國際認證比賽都剛好辦在母親節,邱月香自然而然地成了孩子們口中的「邱媽」。

曾任外交及國防委員會的立法委員陳歐珀出身宜蘭,授旗時說道:「要是這次宜蘭的孩子能得到冠軍,我就跟著孩子們叫妳『邱媽』!」會場中,陳歐珀私下問了邱月香為什麼要這般付出?邱月香回他:「為了弭平數位落差,讓台灣可以跟世界接軌,讓我們的孩子在未來的十年、二十年能跟別人一較長短!」而那次比賽,宜蘭的孩子真的為邱媽掙贏了臉面,拿了冠軍回來!當台灣的孩子載譽歸國,在記者會的現場,陳歐珀一進來就跟著大家宏亮地叫了——「邱媽好!」

● 揹著國旗，我現在要出征

　　「每次出國時，孩子們總會自發性地拿兩面國旗，插在背包上，好像三太子要出征一樣。」邱月香感動地說：「很奇怪，沒有人教他們，但他們都這麼做，每當得了獎，就像變魔術一樣，孩子們就從背包裡拿出大國旗拉開照相，熱情地親吻著國旗，還有人會把國旗披在身上開心的又叫又跳。」拭去眼角的淚水，既是驕傲又是感動。透過邱月香的眼眸，台灣的未來在國際舞台上散發著無比的光芒。那十二道光的溫暖，光榮地照耀在每一個台灣人身上。

邱月香鼓勵選手們多與國際選手交流，日後會成為台灣資訊產業的新血與活力！

每每在競賽中獲獎，選手們一定會拿出身上的國旗，驕傲地告訴全世界：「我們來自台灣！」

資安教母

不計心力推動資安立法

資安教母：連結駭客與政府的橋梁

　　在與國外的接觸中，邱月香發現國際會議上常常提到Security（資安）、Privacy（隱私）。這讓她對資安有了初步的認識。在與國際接軌的教育訓練中，又認識了台灣的小駭客，台灣早期的駭客年會，都是靠著熱血的年輕人在經營苦撐，每當小駭客們來向邱媽請求協助，向來支持電腦教育的邱月香便毫不猶豫地贊助，還不忘叮囑他們要當破解惡意攻擊的「白駭」，不要當網路犯罪的「黑駭」！

　　有一年的駭客年會，長期支持資安活動的邱月香站在台上演說，很早就與世界接軌的她提出：希望台灣能成為「Security Island」（資安島嶼），擁有一流軟體人才的台灣，可以藉此成為各國的安全智庫。影響所及，甚至連當時的總統府高層都請邱月香牽線，邀請駭客們到總統府會談。

　　邱月香微笑地說：「那些小駭客們都是用代號而不用本名，見到政府官員也都不換名片的！」可是，當邱月香與駭客們對話時，親切又響亮的「邱媽」不時從對話中流出，顯見邱月香在小駭客的心中，是「正港」的台灣資安教母！

邱月香與小駭客們合影，並鼓勵他們要當破解惡意攻擊的「白駭」

● 《資安人》—— 共推資安的好夥伴

　　《資安人》，是國內第一份將資安當做專題報導的雜誌，看到了《資安人》雜誌後，邱月香立刻讚嘆：「台灣也有人跟我一樣，開始重視資安了！」在此機緣下，與《資安人》總召集人侍家驊成為好友。侍家驊感動地說：「在我們成立之前，台灣已有一群人在努力關注這個領域。我們跳出來做媒體，大家就自然而然地把觀點和想法跟我們交流互動。」在韓國、新加坡、甚至中國，都已經要求把身分識別做好，這是一項進步的政策；但台灣當時，並沒有一個相關的立法機關在處理，只有一個資通安全會報。侍家驊認真地說：「進入資安領域，才發現有網軍自由進出政府的機密資料庫，這是外界看不到的，這不單單是企業裡的資訊安全問題，更會影響社會安定、國家安全！」

有請 FBI 演講，全力宣導資安

當時瞭解資安的人不多，邱月香引進國外電腦專家、還請 FBI 資安相關人員來台演講。邱月香用最淺顯易懂的方法，對這些上市櫃的公司老闆們提出平易簡單的說明：「公司的電腦資料庫就像一間房子一樣：在不知不覺中，房屋漏水了，樹枝伸進來，房子完全被外界『看不見的敵人』給入侵，這些侵入者就叫『駭客』，在網路的世界裡，我們一定要防範於未然！」

邱月香邀請 FBI 電腦專家來中國科技大學分享資安的重要性

從 2007 年起，邱月香請專家每月寫一篇有關於資安的文章，但這一類的報導對一般讀者來說過於生硬。侍家驊打趣地形容：「資安對一般人來說，就像唸文言文一樣難懂，但邱月香卻想了一個非常簡單的方法，讓更多人容易瞭解。」邱月香笑著說：「其實，就是用四格漫畫的方式，讓大家容易閱讀資安文章的內容。」就這樣，每篇文章搭配著一則生動活潑的四格漫畫，在《資安人》連載。侍家驊肯定地表示，因為這樣的推廣，讓台灣愈來愈多的人知道資安的重要，台灣實際從事資安的人進步非常大！這也是邱月香的真知灼見！

● 推動立法：立法院開記者會

2010 年 4 月，個人資料保護法在立法院三讀通過，經過多年的努力，所費的精力與金錢不計其數，邱月香依然覺得當時的法條還不是很完善；「但至少對台灣來說，已是很大的進步！」今日的國發會主秘何全德，清楚地知曉邱月香在個資保護法上的付出與重要，當下就對邱月香說：「邱媽，妳真了不起！」但邱月香和侍家驊清楚的知道：在台灣資安的路上，還需要更多的努力和奮鬥。

熱血駭客的理想與現實

以往在資安界學習到的專業技術，對於收入來說，並沒有實際幫助，所以大家都是用熱情在增進實力，但「興趣」並不能得到相對應的薪水，曾經有位很有名的駭客告訴侍家驊：「我要結婚了，可能沒辦法再鍛鍊駭客技術了。」侍家驊十分惋惜地說，成為駭客是那個人的理想，但結婚養家卻是他的責任，當現實生活中這兩者相互抵觸、無法相輔相乘時，就表示台灣資訊產業觀念落後，出了很大的問題！

邱月香說，那位駭客結婚後，在她的辦公室裡創業，她還介紹不少工作給他們。有一次國發會帶他們去拉斯維加斯開會，國發會委婉地表示他們沒這個預算，當下邱月香就直接表態：「沒關係，我搞定！」

「吸引年輕的人才不難，一個是成就感，一個就是薪水。」同樣用熱情在做資安的侍家驊有感而發地說：「台灣的人才教育好了，但就業市場卻還沒有這樣的危機意識。在國外，資安是一種風險轉移的保護工作，但反觀國內，預防的觀念還不夠，對資安的投資重視度不足。網路世界裡高手比比皆是，一旦企業的資安出了事情，該如何幫忙？如何解決？怎麼排解難題？所以，台灣的資安觀念一定要有革命性的改變。」

成為阿碼科技的天使投資人

2013 年,阿碼科技(Armorize)被全球知名郵件加密大廠、美國上市公司 Proofpoint,以 2,500 萬美元(約新臺幣 7.5 億元)收購,創下台灣軟體公司被併購的天價紀錄!但是,當阿碼科技成為炙手可熱的科技新貴前,還有一段不為人知的往事。

早期台灣政府網站常常是中國網軍鎖定攻擊的目標,中國駭客在網站植入惡意程式後,只要有人瀏覽被攻擊的網站,就會被惡意程式植入到瀏覽者的電腦。2005 年,阿碼科技創辦人看見了台灣資安的迫切需求,開啟了創業之路。然而在台灣做軟體創業很難,資安創業更難!當時的創辦人黃耀文向素來支持資安的邱媽商量,希望能相互投資,深知資安重要的邱媽,二話不說就答應了黃耀文,成為了阿碼科技創業初期的天使投資人。

阿碼科技也不負眾望,幾年之內便成為台灣解決網路安全的重要新創業者,更為國際大廠所青睞。這也更加證明了邱月香所言——台灣的確有實力可以成為「Security Island」,各國的安全智庫!

資訊力即國力，資安即國安

　　蔡英文總統上台後喊出——「資訊力即國力，資安即國安」。邱月香表示：「2015 年總統選舉前，中華軟協舉辦的資訊軟體與服務產業發展建言，當時的主題就是這兩句。」邱月香邀請了當年的總統候選人蔡英文出席，「我告訴他們一定要『Change mindset and innovation』（改變思維和創新）」。正因為邱月香對資安的倡議與重視，蔡英文總統上台後推動國防科技產業，邱月香便成為唯一的民間代表。

● 創造產業，功成不居

　　頗有遠見的邱月香，知道資訊安全將來一定會成為全球資訊產業的必備顯學，為此，在 2007 年，就先創辦了台灣隱私權顧問協會（TWPCA），並邀請當時的關貿網路總經理陳振楠擔任理事長；自己再成立台灣個人資料保護協會（TWPDA），與《資安人》攜手把資安的議題打響！「我們打造了台灣第一個資安產業！」邱月香豪氣地說：「當年要不是我們一起把這個產業推向舞台，台灣可能還沒有人重視資安呢！資安這一塊是我一手喊上去的！」

　　她還對當時是行政院研考會資訊管理處處長、今日的國發會主祕何全德建議推動台灣的駭客「道德認證（CEH）」[5]，在全力與侍家驊推動資安立法後，邱月香卻選擇隱身幕後，她說自己的階段性任務完成了，要讓更適合的人去好好發揮。而她自己為台灣資訊產業升級的願望，從未停歇！

---

[5] CEH 是 Certified Ethical Hacker 的簡稱，在業界稱之為道德駭客認證，CEH 這門課，主要介紹駭客常用的工具及攻擊方法，從中實際了解駭客行為及其思維模式，進而知道如何保護網路安全、強化系統免受攻擊，防堵不法駭客的入侵。Ethical Hacker 是指行為合乎道德倫理規範的駭客，因此有人稱 CEH 為白帽駭客認證，希望與違反道德倫理規範的怪客（Cracker）做區別。

活躍社交與
溫柔心靈

會見達賴——慈悲與智慧之旅

「我要做的事，很少有做不到的。」邱月香自信地說：「我會想盡一切的辦法，將問題一一克服！」意志力超強的邱月香如此表示：「就算老天爺再怎麼想幫你，你沒那個『GUTS』跨出去也做不成！」在她堅定的意志貫徹下，那看似不可能的任務她一一完成了。

2001 年 3 月底，達賴喇嘛來台進行為期十天的「慈悲與智慧之旅」。達賴喇嘛曾表示，他唯一想會見的女性，只能是一位「非常重要」的女人！所有人都認為應該是當年的副總統呂秀蓮。就在其她女性都被拒於門外之時，邱月香想盡辦法找人幫忙，最終透過朋友的牽引，在達賴喇嘛還沒演講之前，就得以與他合影留念。

邱月香與達賴喇嘛合影

扶輪社團體研究交換

　　看著邱月香資歷上一長串的經歷與活動：從行政院顧問、資策會常務董事到樂團顧問；從政治到資訊產業，從資訊產業到藝術演出，她經營生涯的跨領域程度令人瞠目結舌！在眾多組織的領導者與顧問中的社交經驗裡，最令她印象深刻，影響最為深遠的活動，邱月香給了一個與眾不同的答案。

　　「扶輪社 GSE，Group Study Exchange。」

　　參加扶輪社超過 30 年，提攜無數後進的國際扶輪 3480 地區前總監 Medicare 說明什麼是 GSE：

　　「國際扶輪基金會在 1965 年，為了培養年輕的專業人士，在全世界五百三十幾個地區進行團體研究交換計劃（GSE），出訪團到外國的配對地區交換訪問，由於組成的團員都是專業人士，除了可以體驗異國的生活方式，還可參訪與本身職業相關的專業機構。」Medicare 總監邊說，邊拿出邱月香當年的名片：「她真的是十分稱職的團長，在她的團員裡還有一位現任中央廣播電台台長。第一次見到她是在芙蓉扶輪社授證當天，她是創社秘書，當時我心想：在這麼大的一個女性社團會被大家推派為祕書，一定不是偶然！」

　　這是扶輪社常年的例行活動，與不同國家進行交換訪問，2001 年為期三十五天的參訪，邱月香和團員們分別到美國喬治亞州的社友家中，眾人要在短暫時間內推廣台灣，讓對方瞭解台灣的文化。因此所有

邱月香與 GSE 團員到美國喬治亞洲進行 GSE 文化交流

人無不戰戰兢兢，把這次參訪當成人生的第一次、也是最後一次的異國交流而全力以赴！每次在接待社友所屬的扶輪社演講，演講的內容都必須在前一晚的腦力激盪中討論擬定。有時面對演講的群眾更多達四、五百人，站在台上，邱月香笑著說緊張到心臟幾乎都快跳了出來！

但就算 GSE 的行程緊密，邱月香還是每天收獲滿滿！「我特別在教育內容及課程上花了很多心力去研究他們的運作，也參訪了當地的教育機構 Kennesaw State University，與校長 Dr. Betty Siegel 一同參與 Possible Woman Leadership Conference，與來自全美各界優秀的女性相互交流，受益良多，就連當地的媒體都有報導。」邱月香興奮地拿出當

時的合照與報導：「2002 年，我帶孩子們出國比賽時還特地包車繞過去喬
治亞州，將我走過的路分享給孩子們。竟然還巧遇到去年參訪時認識的當地
扶輪社社友！他還驚訝地問我：『Yvonne, why you are here!』」海內存知己、
天涯若比鄰，正是此刻最佳的寫照。

Betty Siegel 是美國喬治亞
州著名的教育家，在 2001
年舉行的 Possible Woman
Leadership Conference 中
為三大主講人之一（左一）

2001 年，邱月香到喬治亞州進行文化交流，特地拜會 Kennesaw State
University 的校長，也是知名教育家 Betty Siegel，針對教育理念進行溝通分享。

與卡特總統的插曲

喬治亞州正是前美國總統卡特的故鄉，參訪團因此得以在教堂裡聆聽卡特的演講，在這難得的經驗中，還有一段意外的小插曲。

「在這間教堂裡，你們每一個人的國家我都去過，對嗎？」卡特自信地說著。

「NO~」當時身為團長的邱月香大聲地回應，現場眾人莫不將眼光移向這位女子，究竟是誰膽敢在前美國總統面前如此直接？

「Where are you from?」竟然有人敢當面說 No ！卡特質疑地看向她。

「I am from Taiwan!」邱月香輕快自信地說。

聽到了 Taiwan，卡特沉吟了半晌，低沉地說了聲：「Yes.」

演講進入了主題，卡特總統當時正在為 NGO「非政府組織」募款，當他問起有誰願意捐獻？邱月香毫不遲疑地高舉起手：「Yes, Taiwan can!」

在眾人驚訝的目光中，她又一次為台灣外交敲出了一記漂亮的全壘打！

演講完畢，卡特與 GSE 團員們集體合照，為此行劃下圓滿的句點，直到今日，邱月香與卡特互動的小插曲，還為團員們所津津樂道。

2001 年在美國參加 GSE 時，邱月香的不卑不亢和慷慨大方，令前美國總統卡特留下了
深刻印象

● 反省：看人不該看膚色

　　那段時間邱月香形容自己每天都在充電，每天都在接受文化衝擊：「有一次在大賣場的停車場進行交換家庭聯誼，有一個團員將被一位高大的黑人給帶走，我很擔心，於是告訴他：你如果不想去他家沒關係。」說到這邱月香睜大了眼，懊惱地說：「我萬萬沒想到，那位高大的黑人竟然是銀行的副總裁！」她嘆了長長的一口氣：「我後來也反省自己，別再有這種先入為主的刻板印象。這是我的錯誤，不應該看人看膚色。」

認真：唯一兩任的 GSE 團長

「2001 年她當 GSE 團長十分稱職，不論是個人魅力的展現，或是她對異國交流的用功、團員的用心都是有目共睹。後來去美國阿拉巴馬州的 GSE，我們再推薦她擔任團長。」Medicare 總監肯定地表示，邱月香對活動的付出與熱情，成功地做了最佳的文化交流與國民外交的示範。

對於扶輪社的活動，邱月香總是不遺餘力的投入，抵達阿拉巴馬後，她更去與她的外國媽媽 Joyce 小聚，重溫當年的和樂時光。她謙和地表示，正因為有 Medicare 總監推薦她擔任兩任 GSE 的團長，每天演講前的腦力激盪，紮實的訓練讓她累積了更多國際場合上演講的實力，成為往後在國際舞台上發聲的重要經驗。

邱月香俏皮地說，每次在 GSE 演講的時候，她都會秀出與達賴喇嘛的合照，每次都引起台下眾人發出既羨又妒的「哇～」的嘆息！GSE 的團員們才驚覺，原來當時邱月香會見達賴喇嘛的用意竟是為此！她大方地分享：「說穿了，這就是一個小技巧。在國際場合的演講上，要是沒有來個『先聲奪人』，怎麼引起眾人的注意、贏得深刻的印象呢？」

溫柔心靈，擇善固執

　　邱月香的行善足跡和WITSA會員國一樣遍及世界，她謙和地說，因為小時候吃過苦，所以更能夠「將心比心」。再加上父母樂於分享的家庭教育薰陶，家裡常常支持弱勢族群：「小時候常看到爸爸遇見鄉下挑菜來賣的人，都乾脆一整籃全買回去，為的就是讓他們可以早點休息。」

　　深受影響的邱月香，也常常一買菜就是一堆，再分給親朋好友，因此常被老公笑說是不是要煮給一百多個人吃。邱月香說，父母常提醒她：「沒錢不行，但錢並非是最重要的事，有能力的時候，一定要幫忙、回饋給社會。」

　　對信仰的虔誠、對善念的堅持，正是這樣的心境，塑造了今日的她，不分海內外，都發自內心、真誠地對待與之相處的每一個人。

人道關懷，振臂一呼

「『博愛』之謂仁，『行而宜之』之謂義。」「奉獻愛心不遺餘力」一直是邱月香為人處事的準則之一，無論是 2014 年的高雄氣爆、或是 2015 年贊助日本國寶級現代刺繡大展、以及捐贈物資給宜蘭縣大同鄉南山國小的偏鄉學童、2016 年尼伯特颱風重創台東，協會發起「0708 台東風災捐款及公益活動」、2018 年花蓮大地震，受害戶需要支援救助等等。

正是這樣人飢己飢，人溺己溺的人道關懷，讓每當各地有需要救助時，邱月香總是率先跳出來號召大家，鼓勵中華軟協上下同事捐款：「絕不能忘記我們的同胞正在受苦！」即使她主席與理事長的職位都是不支薪的，助人優先的邱月香也必將捐款的金額補齊到整數，眼也不眨一下。

印度做公益，根除小兒麻痺

　　在參與了這麼多的公益活動，讓她印象最為深刻的，莫過於印度的「根除小兒麻痺之旅」。在邱月香溫暖的眼底，蘊藏著當年令她化悲憤為力量的往事。

　　「那是扶輪社的公益活動，我們到印度，進行根除小兒麻痺的人道救援，那些孩子患者的腳有的是三角型，有的是圓的……社員積極募款，資助開刀醫療費，希望能讓孩子們的雙腳正常。」說到這她緩緩地嘆了一口氣，語氣中有著難掩的悲傷和不捨。

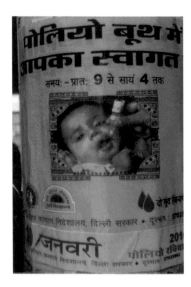

在印度當地張貼由扶輪社
執行的根治全球小兒麻痺
計畫海報，告知當地民眾
踴躍參加

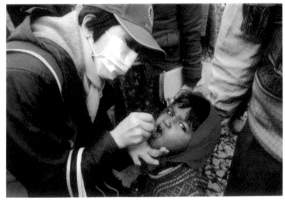

十分景仰比爾蓋茲熱心公益的大愛，邱月香參與由扶輪社執行的根治全球小兒麻痺計畫，前往印度學習人道救援

「那時到印度去參加全國免疫日（NID, National Immunization Day），我們準備了很多禮物，有吃的有用的。那裡人很多、範圍又大，每次拜訪完一個家庭就要做記號，才不會重複醫療，但也因為範圍太大了，扶輪社的社友們就劃分區域，點完藥的孩子就在他的小指甲塗上記號，塗完了就給禮物，他們拿到時都很開心！但印度的生活真的太苦了，有的孩子為了再拿禮物，竟然把指甲上的記號都磨光了……」話音未落，邱月香眼底閃露著點點淚光。

慈悲救人要 TAKE ACTION！

「那時我們住在貧民窟，四周全是垃圾！回來後那渾身的臭味怎麼都清不掉，但一想到那裡的孩子環境居然這麼困苦，就讓我有更多的動力為他們再做下去。」

就在那一刻，這位叱吒國際舞台的 WITSA 主席，化身為降臨印度貧民窟的偉大母親，強忍著眼裡的淚，為孩子們一一點藥，「看到那些孩子在乞討，我心裡明白：就算為他們掉再多眼淚也沒有用！」這句話說得擲地有聲，因為看到孩子們受困於環境，無力擺脫貧窮命運而不忍，更堅定了她要為台灣多做一些事情的決心！

邱月香說：「我常在演講的時候提到把事情做好，需先跟對方 Make friends（成為好友），然後執行、完成這四個步驟：一、Create awareness（規劃藍圖）；二、Lend the hand（伸出援手）；三、Take action（採取行動）；四、Make dream real（讓夢成真）。」正因為有這樣的「成功模式」，讓她面對任何事情都無往不利。她緊握起雙拳，眼睛忽地炯炯有神：「我有信心，一定能讓台灣走出去！」

第六章

WITSA 主席之路

從 CISA 到 WITSA 鏈結台灣與世界

軟體產業首位女性理事長

　　1983 年，中華民國資訊軟體協會正式成立，邱月香在進入中華軟協深耕 12 年後，在協會理監事支持下，2014 年出馬競選中華軟協理事長，面對 3 月即將來臨的選舉，邱月香卻在 2 月打高爾夫球時受了傷，正當大家以為她會因此退出競選，沒想到她竟坐輪椅參選到底，在她的熱情與堅持下，果然成為中華軟協成立 30 多年來第一位女性理事長！正當大家讚嘆連連時，4 月上任的當天更讓眾人訝然！身為新任理事長的她，為了在協會同仁面前展現她帶領協會前進的堅韌決心，以身作則，不惜強忍著身體有如千萬根針刺般地的劇痛，走下輪椅、不拄拐杖、靠著意志力一步一步走向大會演講台。她還自我解嘲一番：「這真的就叫『天將降大任於斯人也，必先苦其心志，「斷」其筋骨……才能曾益其所不能』呀！」

　　那時在國賓飯店就職，邱月香形容，她每爬一層階梯，都痛到快昏厥過去，撐到最後一步時才勉強扶搭住演講台：「我告訴自己，今天，我不能輸！」即使冷汗早已沁溼了衣服，也不讓人看出她絲毫的不適，展露笑容，振奮鼓舞的言詞伴隨著眾人驚訝的氣勢，引得台下的同仁掌聲連連！這真是不折不扣客家人的「硬頸精神」！

前瞻思維、跨業合作

「當我第一次當選理事長時，很多人都好奇地問：『妳懂電腦，妳懂軟體嗎？』我心中很不服氣。於是上任後花了四個月的時間，將整個軟體產業更通盤的了解。然後，我提出一個足以翻轉產業的前衛想法——跨業、跨界、跨國！」

什麼是「跨業」？軟體開發本來就可以因不同行業、不同需求而研發。什麼是「跨界」？例如設計、工程、醫療、建築、軟硬體……不同領域也可相互支援。什麼是「跨國」？當新軟體開發出來後，國和國之間可以互通有無、相互交流，以科技促進人類進步！這正是未來世界的趨勢，如此翻轉產業，令人耳目一新的見解，讓台灣軟硬體界無人不識邱月香！

● 提升軟體產業，全國一起來

社會上普遍對於軟體開發業有誤解：台灣的硬體公司有大型廠房、有漂亮成品，舉世聞名；但軟體開發在數量和質量上反而不見起色，市場規模和人力需求也不成正比，在籌措資金上相對困難。因此，不少軟體開發業者求助於邱月香，希望她能代表軟體產業向政府相關單位發聲，給予更多的幫助。邱月香也感慨，儘管她也向有關單位反應過，但政府中仍有許多人真的看不懂軟體產業的前瞻性；「2000 年後矽谷靠軟體轉型，政府一定要有人深入瞭解軟體這項創新產業，從內需市場帶動外需市場……台灣需要的應該不是像矽谷的『純軟體』產業，而是一個『軟體應用』產業，如同我提出的跨業、跨界，結合軟體和各專業產業的人才，才能打造讓自己驕傲的軟體應用環境，因為，台灣其實是非常有實力的！」

● 合作：從熟悉雙方開始，創造雙贏

上任中華軟協理事長後，在一場進行台日合作的致詞上，邱月香就先展現出她不急不徐、為彼此創造雙贏的合作模式：「第一年我們先 make friendship、第二年我 take action、第三年我們 will make dream come true！」不急功近利的氣度贏得日方的尊重。有一回富士通副總裁上台演講時，便引用了這三句話，更說了「This three sentences come from Yvonne」。

WITSA 前主席慧眼識英雌

　　2014 年，上任 CISA 理事長的邱月香，代表 CISA 出席 WITSA 在墨西哥瓜達拉哈拉（Guadelajara）的會員大會，一下飛機便直奔會場的邱月香，因為時差的緣故在會場托腮小憩，殊不知第一次見到她的 WITSA 主席 Sandiego，早已悄悄地關注了這位人小氣勢高的東方女性。

2014 年，第一次擔任 CISA 理事長的邱月香，參加墨西哥瓜達拉哈拉的 WCIT 世界科技資訊大會

兩人熟稔後，Sandiego 告訴邱月香第一次在大會上見到她時，心中便興起了一個念頭：「I saw you. You are the one!」不解的邱月香反問他：「One for what?」Sandiego 反而先表明：「我想了解一下台灣的政治」，向來熱心的邱月香二話不說，立馬安排當時身為 WITSA 主席的 Sandiego 與台灣朝野人士會面。

　　當 Sandiego 見到當年是民進黨秘書長兼駐美代表的吳釗燮時，出乎意料地說：「她（指邱月香）很適合出來競選 WITSA 主席。」當時的邱月香壓根沒想過，只覺得這是一句玩笑話。但知悉邱月香這多年來，在軟體界努力深耕的吳釗燮立刻贊同：「當然，我相信她的競選，會是一件很棒的科技外交！」這下，她才明白，什麼是「One for what」！

　　在兩人的鼓舞下，2015 年 3 月，決定去澳洲坎培拉參與競選，出發宣誓前，邱月香拜會了時任行政院副院長的張善政，更是獲得大力支持！在朝野兩黨共同的力挺下，邱月香決定放手一搏。

在前 WITSA 主席 sandiego（右）的邀約下，邱月香安排他與當時的駐美代表吳釗燮（左）見面，三人並暢談日後台灣與 WITSA 的合作與科技外交

女力崛起：當選 WITSA 主席

當時已成功為台灣爭取舉辦 2017 WCIT 的邱月香，身為 CISA 理事長的她，開始了邁向國際組織 WITSA 的主席之路。

緊接著，忙碌於全球會員的拜會、聯繫和競選準備，在前主席的協助下，2016 年 10 月 2 日在巴西，由超過 83 個國家的資訊與通訊同業團體、全球最大的資通訊服務產業組織——WITSA 世界資訊科技暨服務業聯盟，她——邱月香——成功地當選為首位來自台灣的主席！也贏來了台灣人在聯合國裡的一席之地！

當選 WITSA 主席，至今走遍了 20 幾個國家，會見過各國總統、總理、部長、三軍統帥：「不少人看到東方人又是女性、很多人都不敢相信……，我經常提醒自己：今後要更努力、更勇敢、不畏難，碰到事情時，要更敏銳、快速地處理好。」雙手輕放在沙發扶手，邱月香回想這兩年來的點點滴滴，小心、謹慎正是她一路走來成功的不二法門，她的當選，亦象徵著世界「女力崛起」的新趨勢，也代表著台灣在全球資訊產業界上的肯定！

2016 年 10 月 2 日在巴西,邱月香擔任超過 83 個國家的資訊與通訊同業團體、全球最大的資通訊服務產業組織 WITSA 主席,也是首位來自台灣的主席!

在邱月香的力爭下,台灣果然如願接到 2017 年 WCIT 的主辦權!

改變章程，爭取 WCIT 在台灣舉行

資訊界奧林匹克——世界資訊科技大會（WCIT）向來為雙年一辦，2016 年已確定由巴西主辦，2018 年更有四個國家出面爭取！2014 年，第一次擔任 CISA 理事長的邱月香，在參加墨巴哥瓜達拉哈拉舉辦的 WITSA 大會上，知道在這樣的情勢下，台灣最快也要 2020 年才有機會。邱月香靈機一動，向來多智機敏的她，立刻拋出一枚前所未有的震撼彈：「科技隨時在進步，WITSA 是國際的科技組織，應該要一年一辦，不然，我們根本跟不上時代！」話音一落，現場掌聲如雷一致通過！

在順利說服大會改變章程，成為每年舉辦的科技盛會後，考量當時已經有四個國家在爭取 2018 年主辦權，WITSA 秘書長告訴邱月香 2019 年可以在台灣舉辦，但她竟然斬釘截鐵地回應：「要辦，就是在 2017 年，因為我們現在有政府的全力支持！預算絕不是問題！」這一段話，成功爭取 WCIT 2017 在台灣。

2015 年邱月香即拜會張善政前院長（當時為行政院副院長），希望爭取 WCIT 2017 在台灣舉辦，曾經擔任 Google 亞洲硬體營運總監、跨足產官學界的張前院長深知 WCIT 的重要性與國際上的影響力，透過國際的專業組織，推展台灣的實力，與各國的串聯更是難能可貴。

「WITSA 不是一個商業導向的組織，就是因為沒有商業性，更能展現台灣優秀的資訊科技實力。」張前院長說道，「舉辦 WCIT，可以讓台灣在國際發聲，增加台灣的能見度，政府沒有不幫的道理！」獲得了張前院長的鼎力相助、周知各部會全力支持，邱月香更是全力奔走國際，為舉辦 WCIT 放手一搏！

為台灣發聲，朝野上下一心

　　這一切的努力，前行政院長張善政皆看在眼裡。他知道，身為協會的主席，不但要解決財務與專業上的困難，更要滿足會員的期待，國際上的奔波與人脈比國內的理事長更難！「然而好事多磨，已經困難的事又碰到了 2016 年政黨輪替。」張前院長說：「台灣的國際空間如此艱困，政府官方管道沒辦法做到的事，如果可以由民間來推展知名度大的國際會議，這個成功模式當然可以作為其他民間組織努力的模範。」

　　邱月香更感恩地說：「當時張院長很大器，他要我寫信給小英總統，希望朝野皆能玉成此事。」邱月香再三強調：「拿到 WCIT 2017 年的主辦時，國際上都很期待看到台灣的能量，我認為既然要辦，我們就要辦到最好，台灣，不能讓人看笑話！」在時間的壓力與諸多不確定下，邱月香多方奔走，在多次與官方溝通後，獲得經濟部長沈榮津的全力支持，又一次，邱月香以己身的真誠，完成不可能的任務！

2015 年，邱月香拜會當時的行政院長張善政，希望能獲得 2017 年 WCIT 台灣主辦權的官方支持。張善政表示，朝野上下全力支持，政府與民間齊心合力，一定要讓全世界看見台灣的科技實力！

WCIT 2017 在台灣

2017 年 9 月台灣成為第一個單年舉辦 WCIT 的國家！蔡總統與邱月香、沈部長、吳政委及贊助大會貴賓們合影

2017 年，台灣，成為第一個單年舉辦 WCIT 的國家！

2017 年 9 月，台北，暌違 17 年、資訊界奧林匹克 WCIT 再度在台舉辦──第 21 屆世界資訊科技大會（WCIT 2017），83 國代表出席，近千位的國外賓客，4,500 多位資訊科技界領袖參與。

10 日，數位夢想大展率先在世貿一館熱鬧登場，產官學研大規模展示超過 680 個攤位的未來科技大展，帶動 B2B 國際媒合交流活動。11 至 13 日，台北國際會議中心舉行 16 場平行會議與活動，勾勒對未來數位夢想的無限想像。

經濟部長沈榮津指出，WCIT 2017 不單是一場三天的國際論壇活動，更是讓世界體驗台灣智慧城市應用的重要契機。這次大會聚集台灣實力大廠及新創公司，展示我國從「資訊硬體代工大國」成熟轉型為「資訊應用數位強國」的重要實力，傳達社會經濟正面新能量。

行政院院長賴清德在 WCIT 晚宴上指出：台灣已訂定國家發展方向，由製造代工轉型為智慧創新領域，要讓台灣成為數位經濟、物聯網、大數據分析、雲端計算、人工智慧等的領導國家。

行政院院長賴清德（左三）與相關部份首長廣下英雄帖，邀請世界各國的資訊科技領域人士，加入台灣數位經濟的行列

日本 USE 公司吉弘京子會長特地前來台灣參加 WCIT 會議，並與邱月香暢談數位科技的未來方向

弭平數位落差：從台灣到全世界

　　11 日，正式展開為期三天的大會，由總統蔡英文、行政院政委吳政忠、經濟部部長沈榮津、台北市市長柯文哲、WITSA 主席邱月香上台致詞，與全球 83 個國家、4 千多位嘉賓一同舉行開幕式。

　　身為 WITSA 的主席，邱月香用英文向全球會員致詞，她強調：「WITSA 所有的會員，來自 82[6] 個國家，他們全是世界上最頂尖的資訊科技領導人，用英文來演講，以實力展現：台灣，絕對可以跟世界接軌零落差！」至此，1996 年那位從汐止出發，拉拔台灣孩子與國際接軌的邱媽，20 年後以其始終如一的真誠，成了台灣與全球 83 個會員國串連的催生人！

　　邱月香漂亮地幫台灣「翻轉產業、媒合國際」，更提出「弭平全球數位落差，讓全球成為數位公民」的藍圖。身為全球組織 WITSA 的主席，邱月香回首過往，不改其志，謙虛地說這是上天給她的任務！

　　「20 年前，我的願望是幫台灣『弭平數位落差』，20 年後，我仍然做相同的事，只是從『台灣』，放眼到『全世界』！」帶著如此的豪情，來自台灣的超級女客前進聯合國！

---

[6] 不丹已於 2018 年 8 月 22 日成為 WITSA 第 83 個會員國。

鳳凰展翅

前進聯合國

為台灣爭取一席之地——
聯合國的 WITSA 女主席

「『Living the digital dream』是我跟 WITSA 秘書長苦思多日後決定出來的 WCIT 的大會標語，也是我接下來要努力的目標！」目光遼遠，邱月香如是說道。

2017 年春，身為國際組織 WITSA 的主席，出席了聯合國 UNCTAD（聯合國貿易和發展會議——United Nations Conference on Trade and Development）的活動，第一次到聯合國的邱月香，看見每個國家的代表都拿著自己國家的牌子，她便開始尋找，但怎麼找也找不到台灣！這時一個人走了過來詢問：「Where you come from?」，邱月香清亮地回他：「Taiwan」，沒想到那人一聽之後，竟用手揮趕她：「Can't be here!」邱月香當下拿出名片說道：「I'm chairman of WITSA!」對方沒料到邱月香除了是台灣人外，還有另一身分——全球最大資通訊服務產業組織 WITSA 主席——立馬道歉雙手引導：「Your seat is over here!」坐上了席位的邱月香不禁感慨台灣今日的國際處境，與此同時，拿起 WITSA 主席立牌的她，心中更升起了要為台灣鏈結世界的決心！

當時在聯合國大樓裡，正舉辦著中國藝術展，而馬雲也剛好在此開記者會，想到早先的遭遇，對照馬雲在記者會上的意氣風發，邱月香不禁嘆道：「要受到國際的重視，光靠民間的努力是絕對不夠的，國家強，台灣未來才有希望！」一路上靠著自己單槍匹馬、串起了連結與支持、拚出一片天的邱月香，握著雙拳、目光炯炯，再次流露了她的真性情。這位愈打壓愈堅毅的超級女客，穩穩地為台灣開啟串連國際的大門。

2017 年，邱月香出席聯合國 UNCTAD 會議

聯合國早餐會 —— 久違的台灣代表

陪同邱月香前去的，還有資深的 WITSA 秘書長 Dr. Jim Poisant，早已熟稔聯合國事務的秘書長，被邀請參與隔日在聯合國頂樓舉辦、只有重要人物才會受邀的早餐會，秘書長希望邱月香能夠參加，這是串連國際大人物難得的機會。

早餐會上，邱月香自我介紹：「I'm WITSA's chairman. I'm from Taiwan.」她並力邀聯合國的貿易和發展會議（United Nations Conference on Trade and Development，英文縮寫 UNCTAD）的秘書長來台灣演講，台灣有很多人才和資源可以幫助需要的國家，但在此時，她也發現只要說出台灣二字時，現場眾人開始眼神飄移，還沒介紹完，一旁竟有人無禮地打斷：「We belong to United Nation.」

邱月香聽聞此語，即使身在聯合國，一向率真的她立馬回應：「Forget about the politics, we are in the industry!」同時身為資策會常務董事的邱月香繼續介紹著資策會，一個曾受惠於資策會的他國代表，也立刻給予正面嘉許。「我講了兩三次台灣都沒人敢回應……」帶著哽咽，看得出真性情的她的心痛：「大家真的不曉得，台灣，在國際上真的很苦……」邱月香臉往上仰，不讓人看出她眼底的淚。

飛翔──台灣的女兒

WCIT 成功落幕，邱月香受墨西哥部長之邀前往墨西哥頒獎，墨西哥的報章大篇幅地報導了這位來自台灣、舉辦了科技界盛事WCIT的女主席！

2018 年 2 月，前往印度參與 WITSA 董事會，身為全球主席的她介紹了電腦公會主辦的 Smart City，力邀各國會員參與。更在一個月內促成了桃園與印度 ICT 產業著名的海德拉巴簽訂產業合作備忘錄，以城市外交的方式快速拓展國際外交。

4 月，邱月香前往日內瓦參與聯合國大會，再次參與聯合國頂樓早餐會報，她笑著說上回已經認識了一些人，今年就比較輕鬆了。WTO 台灣辦公室副主任事後得知，訝異地問她：「妳好厲害，怎麼可以參加那個早餐會報？」在聯合國裡已經結交不少朋友的邱月香笑著說「所幸我是 WITSA 主席，不然連聯合國都走不進去！」

2017 年，邱月香受邀前往墨西哥，與墨西哥交通部長 Gerardo Ruiz Esparza（右二）合影

2018 年 2 月，邱月香受邀前往印度演講，與印度百大影響力人物、世界知名靈性導師大師 Sadhguru（左二）合影

2018 年 1 月在印度記者會上，邱月香與印度泰倫加納省資訊科技廳長拉奧 K.T. Rama Rao（右二）、NASSCOM 會長 Mr.Chandrashekhar（右一）合影，並促成桃園與印度 ICT 產業著名的海德拉巴簽訂產業合作備忘錄

2018 年 4 月，邱月香在日內瓦聯合國經濟圓桌論壇早餐會前留影

　　5 月，邱月香受邀出席 WITSA 會員國希臘 SEPE（Federation of Hellenic Information Technology & Communications Enterprises），於希臘雅典主辦的數位經濟論壇（Digital Economy Forum）參與盛會，在致詞中，她強調，資訊和通信科技（ICT）是全球經濟的主要驅動力，體認這一事實的各國政府，必須將信息通信技術作為所有決策的核心。她指出，WITSA 組織的使命是 Fulfilling the Promise of the Digital Age，希望全世界每個人都能在資訊和通信科技中努力前進。恢宏的氣度以全球為藍圖的擘劃，台下如雷的掌聲久久不止。

　　除了在數位經濟論壇發表演說，邱月香也邀請台灣駐希臘代表郭時南出席 Digital Economy Forum GALA dinner，與希臘總理阿列克西斯‧齊普拉斯（Alexis Tsipras）會面，分享台灣 ICT 產業的進步，希望未來能促成兩國更多經濟與合作關係。

　　接著飛往亞美尼亞，5 月剛接任的新科亞美尼亞總理尼可‧帕西

2018年5月前往希臘，與希臘總理Alexis Tsipras（左一）晤面暢談，希望未來能促成兩國更多商貿往來與合作關係

尼揚（Nikol Pashinyan），在導引國內和平變革取得領導權後，立即拜會俄國總理普丁。回到國內第一個接見的外賓就是——WITSA 邱月香、秘書長 Dr. Jim Poisant 與亞洲辦公室策略長蔡淑賢。會談中新科亞美尼亞總理再三重申，亞美尼亞變革中朝數位科技發展的決心，並邀請邱月香為顧問，希望可以在 WCIT 2019 的主辦後，與台灣一樣，能夠獲得世界的肯定，加入科技領先的潮流。

　　7月，邱月香受邀出席新加坡世界區塊鏈峰會（Singapore World Blockchain Conference），會議以「Next in Blockchain」為主題，探討全球區塊鏈技術與應用的未來趨勢。在演講中，邱月香特別分享台灣目前在協助愛沙尼亞的應用區塊鏈技術的成果：如電子稅務、電子投票、健康紀錄等，使愛沙尼亞成為數位國家的典範。同時也強調：台灣在區塊鏈技術，也已應用於金融、醫療、供應鏈管理、能源交易與供需管理、農業、數位版權及公共管理等，成績斐然。期盼全世界未來在區塊鏈產業上，與台灣有更多的合作。

從墨西哥、印度、希臘、泰國到新加坡，邱月香都運用「先由民間敲門，官方同時接洽」的方式，帶領台灣駐外辦事處人員接觸當地官方單位，讓長久不得其門而入的外交人員，得以與政府高層會晤。也難怪一聽到邱月香抵達當地，駐外辦事處無不熱烈歡迎！

　　「我常想：如果 G20（國際經濟合作論壇）可以串連世界各個重要經濟體，那 ICT20（資訊及通訊科技）的成立，也一定可以成為世界重要的資通訊組織，WITSA 有 83 個會員國，等於有 83 個可以讓台灣與當地政府單位接觸的『非官方機會』，讓台灣成為全世界 ICT 產業的重心，還能在外交上有更實質的深化互動。」

2018 年 5 月邱月香前往亞美尼亞，5 月剛接任的新科亞美尼亞總理 Nikol Pashinyan 見面，暢談國家科技發展

同時，邱月香亦與亞美尼亞總統 Armen Sarkissian 會晤，對於日後資訊科技合作進行交流

Soft Power is Changing the World

　　女性在職場裡的辛苦，身為職業婦女的邱月香更是明瞭，看似一帆風順的她，也在 2017 年競選連任中華軟協理事長時，遭受不少打壓和黑函的攻擊。「當時幾乎每一個身邊的朋友都來勸退，甚至還包括企業界的大老！此外，一位曾與我共事十多年的戰友，跟我說了一個多小時的電話，只為了勸我打消連任的念頭！」

　　即使面對所有排山倒海的壓力，邱月香只用一句話來回覆所有的質疑：「我，邱月香的前途，是掌控在我自己的手裡！」

　　「這或許就是我天生個性上的一種……『韌性』吧。」邱月香雖然嘴角含笑，但眼神依舊充滿著毫不服輸的堅毅：「從我在美國創業時，無論遇到任何困難，我都一定想方設法地解決，不達目的絕不罷休。直到成為中華軟協的理事長、當上了 WITSA 的主席，所遇上的難題更是多如牛毛，我還是一樣的個性，就連醫生也勸我要適時休息，紓解壓力。我回他說我有呀，懂得享受人生，活在當下，這就是我『紓解壓力』的方法。」

　　已是 WITSA 全球主席，邱月香還是維持著自己打理家務的習慣，只要一有空，她一定會逛逛傳統市場，下廚煮飯，尤其是義大利麵和烤無骨牛排更是她拿手絕活！「我無時無刻不提醒自己：要提升自己的能力，什麼事都要會，別人可以，我也一定行！」提升數位教育、幫助女性就業，熱心公益的她深信著—「Soft power is changing the world!」

她也曾當面向蔡英文總統表達「資訊力即國力，資安即國安」的前瞻建言，亦和美國總統民主黨參選人希拉蕊見面分享美台關係的利弊，她說：「當今的女力就是：只要堅持，不達目的絕不罷休—『妳的心態會改變整個世界！』」

邱月香曾當面向蔡英文總統提出「資訊力即國力，資安即國安」的建言

同為女性，邱月香更能瞭解在壓力環伺下的辛苦。她亦曾當面向希拉蕊表達她的欽佩之意，同時也獲得希拉蕊的讚揚與鼓勵。

有人問起邱月香
妳這麼拚是為什麼
「為了我的母親」
妳的母親是誰
「我的母親——是台灣」

Soft Power is Changing the World

I choose to go against the current,

reconnecting Taiwan with the World

———————————

Chiu Yue-xiang

Introduction

More than 4,500 leading figures and experts in the field of Information Technology hailing from 83 countries crossed great distances to gather in Taipei on September 10, 2017. Their mission? To convene for the 4-day World Congress on Information Technology (WCIT 2017) and put their heads together to learn and share ideas pertaining to the latest trends in the IT industry and discuss strategies for future growth and development.

The WCIT might not mean much to the layperson, but to players in the IT industry around the world, the WCIT is the IT equivalence of the Olympics! Furthermore, WCIT 2017 was graced by the presence of nine guest speakers who are all internationally recognized leaders and forerunners of the technological field, including:

1. Alan Marcus, Head of ICT Agenda, Member of the Executive Committee at The World Economic Forum. Speaking on the topic of "The Foundation of the Digital Era", Marcus discussed the evaluation and rankings of internet services in various countries and the integration of ICT services, as well as the impact of both software and hardware development on a nation's competitiveness.

2. Founder and Director of MIT Lab Alex Sandy Pentland shared his views on big data analyses of personal data and how to improve public services and stimulate economic growth.

3. Patrick Thomas from German enterprise Covestro, the leader in the promotion of a circular economy system.

4. Bertrand Piccard, Founder of Solar Impulse.

5. Lee Chih-Kung, Former Minister of Economic Affairs of the Republic of China.

The 3rd, 4th and 5th speakers joined forces to discuss the impacts of circular economies and sustainable development.

6. Japan, shared his views on future trends and innovation in ICT development.

7. Jason Zander, founding father of Azure and Executive Vice President of Microsoft, shared about how the Internet of Things has changed the world.

8. Bill Bien, GlobalHead of Strategy and Marketing for Philips Lighting, analyzed strategies and trends in urban development through a discussion of Green Energy and intelligent technology solutions that are necessary for the growth of Cities of Tomorrow.

9. Setsuhiro Shimomura, Former President at Mitsubishi Electric Corporation talked about why digital factories are considered to be the foundation of Industry 4.0.

The nine V.I.P. speakers did not only share their views on future trends in innovation in the ICT industry, but also their forward-looking paradigms. Through their sharing, we learnt the important role that WCIT plays in determining the direction of future developments in smart lifestyle technology. The WCIT Opening Ceremony and the event itself saw the attendance of high ranking officials such as Taiwan President Tsai Ing-wen, Premier of Taiwan William Lai Ching-te, Minister without Portfolio Wu Tsung-tsong, Minister without Portfolio Audrey Tang, Deputy Minister of the National Development Council Tseng Shu-cheng, Minister of Economic Affairs Shen Jong-chin, and Mayor of Taipei Ko Wen-je. Of particular note was the four-day "Taiwan, Living The Digital Dream" exhibition, for this special exhibition was the brainchild of the collaboration between different public agencies and various private corporations and organizations. For the first time ever, the public and private sector worked hand in hand to boost and transform industries in Taiwan. The exhibition also showcased Taiwan's ability to integrate its innovations in software development and excellence in systems design in recent years. Taiwan is now ready to show the world the accomplishments it has achieved in its metamorphosis into a "Digital Nation, Smart Island"!

Who was the person responsible for bringing this landmark ICT event back to Taiwan after a long hiatus? Who was responsible for showing the world that Taiwan has successfully transformed from a nation powered by its OEM industry to a technological superpower with an ICT expertise?

Who is the mastermind behind the scenes?

It all started in 2016, when Yvonne Chiu Yue-Xiang was elected as the Chairperson of World Information Technology & Services Alliance (WITSA), making her the first Taiwanese ever to assume the role of WITSA Chairperson. As the new Chairperson, she convinced the committee to amend its charter to make the formerly-biennial WCIT an annual event and even won Taiwan the hosting right for the upcoming WCIT.

Hence, in 2017, Taiwan became the first country to host the WCIT in an odd-numbered year! In December that very year, WITSA set up its Taipei office. Yvonne Chiu had been on the go right from the first day she became Chairperson, meeting important figures in both the political and business spheres and bringing about enhanced international cooperation. She also took part in a United Nations Economic Roundtable session to show the world Taiwan's relentless pursuit of "Digital Diplomacy and Integrated Marketing"!

This is the story of a woman from Taiwan: a story of her humble childhood growing up in a Hakka family, a story of her diligence and hard work that got her a chance to make a career for herself in the United States, a story of how she earned a spot on the international stage, and how she became a leader in connecting Taiwan to the state-of-the-art technological advances in the world. Soft power is changing the world. Let us now join her on this journey as she shares her inspiring story with us.

Creating new value for Taiwan through innovation, breakthroughs, and opening new doors

Stan Shih, Founder of Acer Inc. and Chairman of Stans Foundation

The Information Service Industry Association of R.O.C. (CISA) was founded in 1983 when I was just newly elected as the Chairperson of the Taipei Computer Association (TCA). Back then, Taiwan's IT industry was only in its budding stage. During my stint as the TCA Chairperson, I shifted the focus of TCA from the domestic market to an international one. The massive international IT industry was growing, and this led to the rapid growth of Taiwan's IT industry as well.

However, CISA was still focusing on the rather limited domestic market at that time. Furthermore, people generally placed more emphasis on hardware development than on software development. Thus, funds allocated to software development took up just a minor part of the overall budget. In addition, the government, who is our biggest client, gave the Institute for Information Industry priority to take up information services projects, so it was very difficult for private IT companies to scale up, and this in turn limited the amount of value that private corporations could create.

It was not until recent years that information services became ubiquitous in our society, and consumers' demand for quality software increased. Therefore, the next key challenge that Taiwan faces would be how its software industry can develop and create value by building upon the foundation of its internationally acclaimed hardware industry.

Besides the favorable market conditions, bringing about growth in the software industry also requires a whole new paradigm. To boost international sales, Taiwan industry players had to start from meeting local demands. The domestic market was the best testing ground for various information application

Stan Shih, Founder of Acer Inc. and Chairman of Stans Foundation, was invited to speak at the 2018 Information Service Industry Strategy Conference organized by CISA in August 2018. Yvonne Chiu presented him with a token of appreciation.

services, for Taiwanese companies to first hone their craft locally before reaching out into the world. The integration of software and hardware would then elevate Taiwan's standing in the international IT industry.

Yvonne Chiu shares many of her personal ideas in this book, many of which echo my own views. I especially admire how she took up the mantle of the WITSA Chairperson and elevated Taiwan's global visibility. Her passion and innovation also helped transform CISA and brought it to a new height.

CISA organized the Information Service Industry Strategy Conference on August 28, 2018. Prior to the event, Yvonne Chiu invited me to sit down with her to discuss the direction that the conference should take, and also asked for my help in inviting some of the speakers. The objective of the conference was to come up with ways to transform the industry through innovation in line with the government's "Five Plus Two" Innovative Industries Plan. The dual themes of the conference were "Cultural Technology" and "Smart Cities and Villages" respectively, and I spoke on "Building Smart Cities and Villages, Developing an Asian Silicon Valley" at the event.

I believe that this approach is both forward-looking and pragmatic; it is where the future lies, and thus it is the direction in which Taiwan's IT industry should work towards. However, in order to realize this vision, we would need governmental policies to help us boost local market demand so as to create a platform for industry players to showcase their innovation. Also, after local companies have honed their skills in the Taiwanese market, they can then enter the international market and contribute to the world as representatives of Taiwan.

I trust that both CISA and WITSA will continue to play pivotal roles in the development of the IT industry in Taiwan under the leadership of Yvonne Chiu. Chiu writes about her hopes for the future in her book, and I for one cannot wait to see what the future holds. It is my hope that we can continue to create ever-increasing value for Taiwan.

How I see Yvonne Chiu: An open-minded person, touching hearts both domestic and abroad with her earnestness

Interview with Ben Wan, President of Acer Inc.

Upon stepping into Ben Wan's office, one is greeted by the sight of mountains of documents piled high on a desk, Chinese calligraphy tools laid out immaculately by the window, and graceful calligraphy works on display, crystallizations of the wisdom of sages past. I was at the Taipei office of Acer Inc. to visit its President Ben Wan, who is also one of the Executive Directors of CISA. Ben Wan sat tall and poised in the office, like a gentleman straight out of a classical portrait.

● Earnestness and Out-of-the-box Thinking

This veteran of the IT industry was full of praise for Yvonne Chiu's accomplishments in CISA. "In CISA, everyone is frank and earnest," he said, "All of us share a common goal, which is that Taiwan's IT industry can attain greater heights both locally and globally as we achieve breakthroughs in our work. Taiwan's economy was built upon a reliance on hardware development. CISA wanted a leader who could think out of the box in order to bring us fresh perspectives, so we elected Yvonne Chiu, whose background sets her apart from the rest of the candidates. It was truly a pleasant surprise for us when we saw that her hard work, dedication, and innovative ideas exceeded all expectations.

Her earnest approach to running the organization turned CISA into a warm family. Home is where one speaks his mind. Everyone, ranging from our co-workers, Taiwan's public agencies, or friends from overseas, is touched by Yvonne's warmth. The care and concern she shows to people around her is extraordinary. At the same time, she is extremely open-minded and is willing to take advice and suggestions from various parties."

- Drawing on the strength of each individual turning CISA into a family

A wise leader sees each employee as an asset and brings out the best in them.

"Great lessons from ancient writings can still be applied to modern lives. '30 spokes connect to a hub, which can connect to an axle due to its hollow nature; the hollow hub is what allows a carriage to run. Containers can serve their function because they are hollow; rooms can be rooms because of the space within.[1]" These are words of wisdom from Laotzu, reminding us that only by emptying ourselves can we absorb goodness. It is precisely Yvonne Chiu's open-mindedness that allows her to bring out the collective wisdom of the team, which then informs the goals of the organization. CISA was already a respectable organization with disciplined members even before Chiu became its Chairperson, but Chiu built on this foundation and brought it to greater heights."

- Breaking through: A display of fortitude and integrative ability

Ben Wan gave a clear example of how Chiu exhibits "out-of-the-box thinking", "She overcame all odds in 2017 and successfully campaigned for Taiwan to host the 21st WCIT!"

---

[1] Ben Wan quoted from Chapter 11 of *Tao TeChing* by Laotzu. Laotzu was a Chinese philosopher who lived in the 6th-century BC. The excerpt emphasizes the fact that "emptiness" is what gives certain objects their functions, and that we ought to embrace this trait in our lives as well, for only by emptying out our preconceptions and ego can we take in new wisdom and knowledge.

"Chiu gave Taiwan a chance to shine internationally. With the infrastructure in place, innovation and creativity have to keep up, or else the international relations we have built over the years would have all been for naught. Today, every country wants to build smart cities and develop better AI technology. The people of Taiwan are very entrepreneurial, and its government is supportive. Furthermore, SI companies in Taiwan are a force to reckon with, and they have the domestic market to use as a testing ground for their innovations. Hence, we see that Taiwan is ready, be it in terms of its hardware industry, software industry, service industry, or its ability to innovate, and CISA possesses the means to integrate all of the above. If Taiwan is able to showcase its edge in these areas on the international stage that Chiu has created for us at the helm of CISA, the world can then get a glimpse of Taiwan's soft power."

Ben Wan's hearty laugh as he analyzed Taiwan's standing in the world is the perfect embodiment of the bright future of Taiwan's ICT industry!

Yvonne Chiu in my eyes: A lady unconfined by stereotypes, and the first female Chairperson of CISA

Interview with Chung Liang-chuan, Chairman of Gjun Inc.

Gjun has been at the forefront of Taiwan's computer education industry for more than three decades now, and the company has trained countless computer experts since its inception. Gjun founder Chung Liang-chuan, who is also one of the Executive Directors of CISA, has witnessed the growth of the software industry in Taiwan over the years. On this day, we have come to Gjun's Taipei headquarters, situated at Gongyuan Road, to speak to this figurehead of Taiwan's computer education industry.

● The first Chairwoman — embracing diversity

Upon meeting Chung Liang-chuan for the first time, one is struck by his hearty laugh, friendly smile, and confident demeanor.

Chung Liang-chuan said candidly, "I have been part of CISA for 22 years, and Yvonne Chiu is the first female Chairperson that CISA has seen. She has been 100% dedicated to her job since the first day." Like the man of business that he is, Chung went right to the heart of the issue, "Yvonne Chiu is the 7th CISA Chairperson since CISA's establishment more than 30 years ago. Personally, I have known her for about 16 or 17 years, and have seen her serve the Computer Society of the Republic of China (CSROC) in the capacity of the Vice Chairperson. Her talents and grit led CISA to invite her to join its ranks. Back in those days, the software industry was dominated by men with engineering backgrounds. However, despite the fact that Yvonne Chiu was not an engineer, she possessed a wide repertoire of knowledge and experience, and had the ability to find the perfect balance of grace, intellect, and empathy. Her assimilation of these diverse traits give her the ability to infuse CISA with a new synergy."

● Bringing together the best of all worlds: Bringing CISA from Taiwan to the world

Chung Liang-chuan's hands moved in sync with his excitement, and he reminded people of an accomplished Chinese warrior, "This is the 5th year that Yvonne Chiu has served as the Chairperson of CISA. She has changed the face of the entire ICT industry in Taiwan and transformed it into something new. Also, because of her great interpersonal skills, she has the support of politicians no matter which party they are from; she even shares positive relationships with the President and various Ministers. Of all the Chairpersons CISA has seen, Yvonne Chiu is the one who has soared to the greatest heights during her time in office! Furthermore, as the Chairperson of WITSA, Yvonne Chiu has led CISA beyond Taiwan's shores and introduced it to the rest of the world. CISA's breakthrough at achieving increased international visibility was made possible by Yvonne Chiu's passion, unique personality traits, outstanding language skills, as well as her ability to connect with people." When it comes to anecdotes about Yvonne Chiu, Chung Liang-chuan recounted fondly, "She is an extremely open-minded and accepting person who is willing to consider suggestions and advice even if they go against her own ideas. It is precisely her willingness to listen to different opinions that allowed her to bring together the best of all worlds and attain new heights in the capacity of CISA Chairperson."

● Bottom-up approach in talent recruitment

When it comes to the issue of "diversity", Chung Liang-chuan mentioned Yvonne Chiu's insistence on adopting a bottom-up approach when it comes to growing the ICT industry, "In the past, CISA placed its focus on how to grow Taiwan's software industry. After Yvonne Chiu became the Chairperson, she organized school visits and sharing sessions to allow tertiary students to learn more about CISA, as she believes that a bottom-up approach like this is the way to attract top talents to join the software industry, and by extension, the way to infuse new blood and energy from diverse backgrounds into the industry as a whole. This switch in approach was not motivated by any profit-seeking desire, but guided by a service orientation to bring CISA to greater heights through the

recruitment of new CISA members from diverse backgrounds. Her personality made this switch appear matter-of-course, but it was actually an enormous breakthrough and revolution in the industry."

● Picking herself up after a fall — a manifestation of her resilience

"CISA has an electoral system for the role of Chairperson, and for Yvonne Chiu to run for Chairperson from her previous role as an Executive Supervisor in the committee, she was effectively looking to take up a job several levels above her. The mere fact that she was willing to step up to serve the organization is a display of her ambition and conviction."

Chung Liang-chuan also shared a story that illustrates Yvonne Chiu's extraordinary fortitude, "During the CISA electoral period, Yvonne Chiu suffered a fracture on her hip joint due to a fall she took while doing sports. Her injury required surgery, but she insisted on chairing the meeting herself on her first day as CISA Chairperson without any form of aid! A hip injury is a serious one, especially for a woman! On average, a person takes a minimum of six months to recover from such an injury, but Yvonne Chiu regained her mobility in just two months!" Chung Liang-chuan's look of admiration was evident, "One can see what a resilient person Yvonne Chiu is from this incident alone. If she has her mind set on something, nothing can stop her from achieving it. Another candidate might have backed out of the election due to such an injury, but not Yvonne Chiu, and this is exactly the reason why she was chosen as the person to lead both CISA and WITSA."

Chung Liang-chuan hardly repeated anything he said during the interview except for the word "extraordinary", which he used twice. To him, Yvonne Chiu's extraordinary dedication led to her extraordinary accomplishments. She spoke at the United Nations as the Chairperson of WITSA and plays a key role in the international software industry. With Yvonne Chiu at CISA's helm, CISA has now opened new doors in terms of its business connections, business network, and also opportunities to showcase Taiwan's technological achievements. As the Chairperson of WITSA, Yvonne Chiu has also brought the organization across borders and grown its influence.

The Yvonne Chiu that I know: The CISA Chairperson who gives her all for Taiwan

Hsu Mei-li, General Manager of Chuanwei Telecoms

I met Yvonne Chiu in the Jiuyang Society, an NGO that I was a part of for close to 30 years. When I first met her, she had just been elected as the Chairperson of CISA. My impression of her was that she was a really energetic person who extends her warmth to the people around her, as well as to all the things she does. I knew that her company specialized in computer education, and she is hugely dedicated to pushing for greater computer literacy. Her charitable nature led her to invest both money and effort into helping Taiwanese students from elementary schools all the way to universities to take part in competitions held overseas, where they performed commendably in terms of their international rankings. I have also heard that she helped steer some Taiwanese youths back to the right path in cyber security issues by similarly providing them with financial and physical support to start their own businesses or to take part in international ICT tournaments, so that they do not become misguided and turn into unlawful hackers. Yvonne Chiu is indeed like a mother hen who takes care of her flock in whatever way she can.

A few years ago, an unfortunate fall during a golf match caused Yvonne Chiu to suffer a hip fracture, and she had to be hospitalized and undergo an operation. After her discharge, I saw her bearing through her pain and attending many activities and events organized by the Jiuyang Society and CISA on clutches. Such is her dedication to friendship and Taiwan's IT industry! I was so moved by her perseverance! Even more impressively, in spite of her injury, she flew to Mexico to attend the WCIT, a WITSA event. Her sense of mission and determination gave her the strength to continue running for the post of WITSA Chairperson even though many felt that she did not stand a good chance of being elected. Eventually, she was elected despite all odds, becoming the first

Taiwanese person to achieve such an honor in the history of the international ICT industry. Additionally, she successfully secured the hosting rights for the 2017 WCIT on behalf of Taiwan. WCIT is a WITSA event that involves 83 different countries from around the world, and the last time that Taiwan hosted the WCIT was in 2000, a whole 17 years earlier. The world was full of both astonishment and admiration for this legendary lady from Taiwan! In 2017, the WCIT was successfully held in Taiwan, thanks to the effort of both the Taiwanese government and its people, and the resounding success of the event led me to marvel at Yvonne Chiu's interpersonal skills, organization skills, coordination skills, as well as her willpower even more!

The unfortunate truth is that Taiwan is being oppressed right now, and our international maneuvering space is being restricted. However, as the International Chairperson of WITSA, Yvonne Chiu was able to overcome various obstacles and navigate freely internationally. Be it at the United Nations, or in countries with no diplomatic ties with Taiwan, Yvonne Chiu did not face much difficulty in arranging to meet with Premiers, Presidents, or Members of the Cabinet with ICT-related portfolios to tell them more about Taiwan. She spoke on behalf of both the private and public sections to her foreign counterparts to support Taiwan's industries. Yvonne Chiu is indeed a Chairperson at an international level with an international outlook. Even today, as we speak, she is still actively making official visits to various countries around the world. Tapping on Taiwan's domestic strengths and the global platform that she has built personally, Yvonne Chiu constantly seeks out new possibilities for Taiwan's future. Her sense of determination and mission are truly worthy of our applause!

Ms. Chiu's exemplary leadership, and countless achievements

Alexandr Yesayan, Co-founder of Ucom, IUnetworks

It has been an absolute honor for me to work closely with Ms. Chiu over the past years on the organization of the World Congress on Information Technology (WCIT), taking place in Yerevan, Armenia in October 2019. Ms. Chiu's vision, experience, and abundant support have played and continue to play a crucial role in surpassing each milestone leading up to the event.

As the 1st female Chairperson of WITSA, Ms. Chiu's exemplary leadership and countless achievements have been the embodiment of women empowerment. Her strength and resilience in the face of challenges in addition to her remarkable problem-solving ability in a swift efficient and diplomatic manner have been invaluable assets for us in particular whilst requesting the support of different stakeholders to ensure the success of WCIT in Armenia.

As I write this introduction Ms. Chiu has visited Yerevan on three separate occasions. Given her hectic schedule this alone serves as proof of her relentless dedication to every project she's involved in.

I look forward to celebrating Ms. Chiu's many more successes to come.

Yvonne Chiu, Santiago Gutierrez Testimonial

Santiago Gutierrez, Chairman Emeritus, WITSA

I met Yvonne in the turmoil of the WCIT 2014 in Guadalajara, Mexico. She arrived directly from her twenty something hours flight straight to the conferenceroom where the WITSA Board was holding its meeting. She dressed like a company top notch executive and that was a good start for a first impression.

During the meeting, that good impression was confirmed through her interventions and participation in the meeting. She had not met yet most of the Board Directors and suddenly she came forward with an unexpected proposal: she offered to undertake the WCIT 2017 in Taipei City. It was more surprising due to the fact that Taiwan had already celebrated WCIT 2000 in Taipei as well.

That was the beginning of a fruitful career in WITSA and of our friendship.

I would like to congratulate Ms Chiu on becoming WITSA's 1st female Chairman. Her dedication to the spirit of WITSA's vision of *Fulfilling the Promise of the Digital Age*, where everyone, regarding of who they or where they reside receives the benefits of Information and Communication Technology. As the former chairman of WITSA representing the country of Mexico for four years, I know well what effort it took to be selected as WITSA's chairman considering the diversity of cultures and the levels of development WITSA members represent.

The dedication to WITSA that Ms Chiu has demonstrated in the period of time she has held the office of WITSA Chairman (2016-2018) is remarkable. She has unselfishly given her time and energy to work with WITSA members in scores of counties around the globe. It is a very good feeling to know that when I completed my term as chairman a very qualified successor not only stepped in to continue the good work of WITSA but excelled as its chairman.

CONTENTS

Chapter One **First Meeting** — A Chairman in the technology field at a United Nations conference

Chapter Seven **The phoenix takes flight** — Onwards, to the United Nations

Chapter One
First Meeting

A Chairman in the technology field
at a United Nations conference

WITSA office in Taipei

Standing by the window in the WITSA Taipei office, situated along Ruiguang Road in the Neihu district, one could take in the sights of half the city. The office was set up in December 2017 for the World Information Technology and Services Alliance (WITSA), which is made up of various organizations in the IT field from 83[2] different countries. Representatives from these organizations are all leaders in the IT industry, including politicians, entrepreneurs, academics, and members of NGOs. The WITSA is the largest IT organization in the world, and its Chairperson is none other than Taiwan's very own Yvonne Chiu, who is also the Chairperson of the Information Service Industry of R.O.C., also known as CISA.

How did a Taiwanese lady become the leader of such an international organization? How did she overcome all odds, against a backdrop of unfavorable diplomatic circumstances that Taiwan faces internationally, to achieve such an impossible feat? The sheer level of perseverance and faith required to carve out a spot for Taiwan in the United Nations, using its ICT achievements as a doorstop, is unfathomable to many.

---

[2] Bhutan, known throughout the world for being "the happiest country in the world", became the 83rd country to be part of WITSA on August 22, 2018, after Yvonne Chiu made an official visit to Bhutan and extended an invitation to the country's leaders.

First meeting

A visitor to the conference room of the WITSA Taipei office can enjoy a view of the iconic Taipei 101 in the distance. The first time I set foot here was last December, when a press conference was held to announce the opening of the WITSA Taipei office. WITSA members from all over the world were in attendance on that day, and the convergence of multiple cultures in one setting reminds one of a UN event.

Cutting across the main office area, I found myself in front of the Chairperson's office. Her office decor, albeit simple, is elegant; the choice of ornaments exudes an air of innocence. A sophisticated lady sat gracefully on the sofa, her light makeup complemented by the string of iridescent pearls around her neck, softening her regal presence with an air of warmth.

"Please have a seat!" Her voice rang out, accompanied by a genteel smile that reminds one of a crescent moon. The exquisite lady in front of me was none other than the Chairperson of WITSA, Ms. Yvonne Chiu.

The Gentlemen's Club: A computer laboratory for businessmen

In the 1990s, Yvonne Chiu returned to Taiwan from the United States. Upon her return, she found that many Taiwanese people did not even know how to turn on a computer. Yvonne Chiu recognized that the age of computers was fast approaching, and she saw for herself the rapid advancement of technology in other countries. Yvonne Chiu, who wanted nothing but to contribute to the growth of Taiwan, was thus committed to bridging the technological gap between Taiwan and the rest of the world. Such circumstances led Yvonne Chiu to set up the Gentlemen's Club herself.

Yvonne Chiu's time overseas made her more of a patriot than ever before. Her concern and love for Taiwan was evident from her words, "Back then, there were many SME business owners who did not even know how to turn on a computer. I told them, 'A computer-illiterate in today's world is virtually a complete illiterate in the future!'" Her spirit of paying it forward touched the hearts of many. Su Tseng-chang, then-Magistrate of Taipei County, even lauded her as "The Most Beautiful Principal"!

Thus, the Gentlemen's Club officially opened its doors to businessmen and made them students again. As these experienced businessmen worked to elevate their computer literacy, The Gentlemen's Club also became a platform for them to network and learn from one another.

Getting CISA's attention through promoting computer education

Back when Yvonne Chiu was the Vice Chairperson of the Chinese Computer Education Association (CCEA), she was concerned about protecting the rights of private education centers under laws governing professional training. She fought for the rights of these education institutes and requested that the government held a public hearing that was "fair, just, and transparent" before passing related laws. Her negotiation skills got the attention of CISA, and CISA's Executive Supervisor F invited Yvonne Chiu to join CISA insistently. Yvonne Chiu accepted the invitation, and there began her 12 years as an Executive Supervisor of the committee herself.

CISA members refer to Yvonne as their "big sister", but not everyone knows how much Yvonne has given to the organization over the last 12 years! Chung Liang-chuan, 22-year member of CISA and the Chairman of Gjun Inc., which is one of the forerunners in Taiwan's computer education industry, said, "When the laws governing professional training was passed down, many of our members turned to CISA for help. Many of these companies took on government projects, but these projects usually came with high expectations and low pay. As a result, many of them were unable to sustain their businesses and suffered losses; some even folded. After Yvonne Chiu joined CISA, she tapped on her extension professional network to help CISA members secure new businesses."

Yvonne Chiu's experiences overseas gave her new perspectives, which she later tapped on to come up with different ways of approaching matters that set her apart from her peers. Yvonne Chiu's efficiency was remarkable. After she joined CISA, she put in place exclusive services for CISA members, as well as signed CISA up for various charity events, hence creating a different kind of added value for members of the organization. One cannot help but wonder what kinds of trials and tribulations Yvonne has gone through to become the woman she is today, a woman who has even become part of the UN. The story of how Yvonne Chiu used her soft power to change the world has just begun!

Chapter Two

A pearl in the making, a diamond in the rough

A superwoman born out of difficult circumstances

A Hakka family: Loving mom, strict dad

"I grew up in 'Goldfish Hairdresser', situated at number 1616 Zhongzheng Road, Taipei. It was the labor of love of my parents, after my father brought my mother to Taipei all the way from Longtan District, Taoyuan, on a tricycle to make a living. Our family was poor, and we often had to take loans in order to make ends meet. Even as a child, I had to help out at the hairdressing salon by shampooing customers' hair or washing used towels in the shop." Yvonne Chiu had a faraway look in her eyes as she reminisced about her childhood, traveling down memory lane to a time when Taiwan's economy was just starting to take off and people were honest and diligent.

"Knowing that my family was poor, I handed over any money that I got from my scholarships and jobs to my mother immediately upon receiving it. My mother did not go to school and not know a single English word, but she was adamant that I learnt English. Back then, I did not understand why."

Yvonne Chiu broke into a smile, "I didn't know why I had to learn English when I was a child, so whenever my mom asked me what I've learnt in my English classes, I always replied with 'How are you? Fine, thank you.' cheekily." A smile lit up Yvonne's dignified features and turned her back into the sprightly little girl who was so impish around her mother.

"My father was very strict with me." Even though many years have gone by, Yvonne's eyes were still a little downcast when she recalled memories of how strict with her her father was, "Whenever boys called our home, he would always tell them 'Yvonne is not around!' even though I could just be sitting beside him! I was not allowed to go swimming, much less camping." However, deep down, Yvonne understood that her father was so strict with her because he loved her.

Portrait of Yvonne
Chius' whole family

Yvonne recalled the expectations her father had for his children, "When we were little, our dad wanted to make sure that we could speak the Hakka dialect because he felt that it was important for us to know our mother tongue. This was in spite of the fact that back in those days, we were only allowed to speak Mandarin in school, and other dialects were banned. As for my father himself, he was someone who made sure he mastered whatever he set out to learn. He even threatened us half-jokingly, 'After I passed, and you needed something from me, you have to talk to me at the altar in Hakka, or else I will just ignore you.' He also drilled the following point into us, 'You have to be someone with foresight. If you can't do that, at least have the wisdom of hindsight. The worst that could happen is that you possess neither!'"

A walk down memory lane: Tough times in the hair salon

Yvonne Chiu has two older brothers and three younger ones. Growing up in such a huge family meant that resources were spread thin, and the family had to take loans at the start of every school year to be able to send the children to school. Yvonne recalled, "When I was still studying in vocational high school, I sometimes had to rush off to class even before I finished what I had to do in the shop. That made me rather depressed…" Time went by, but the young Yvonne was still caught up in the work of the hair salon. Eventually, she dropped out of school for the sake of her family. At this point in her recollection, Yvonne choked up with sorrow. Furthermore, there were other young apprentices in the hair salon, either Yvonne's cousins or children of family friends. Whenever they made a mistake, Yvonne's mother would just point out their blunder and move on, but if Yvonne was the one who slipped up, her mother would tell her off at the top of her voice. On such occasions, Yvonne would just swallow her tears and press on, letting the sound of running water drown out her unhappiness. The young Yvonne did not understand why her mother would treat her own

Yvonne Chiu has been close to her mother ever since she was young. She invited her mother to visit her in Texas, USA, when she was running a business there.

daughter more poorly than she did others, and it was not until many years later that Yvonne realized her mother did what she did for her own good.

● Words of a monk from the Shandao Temple allowed Yvonne to return to school

One particular day, the door to the shop opened, and a monk from the Shandao Temple entered the shop and said he wanted to have his head shaven. Yvonne was intrigued, but she went about her work as usual. Noticing Yvonne at work, the monk said to her father, "She's such a good girl. She should be in school, instead of helping out in the shop!"

"Later on, my father got into the real estate business despite not having any formal training. He was pretty good at it, and our family became better off. Certain major real estate companies that are still around today have sought my father's advice in those days."

Perhaps the secret to Yvonne Chiu's success lies in the Hakka spirit that is at the very core of her being. She was especially thankful for the chance to become a student again because the opportunity did not come by easily!

As for Yvonne's fluency in English, she has her own hard work and her "parents from another land" to thank!

Life in the West: Culture shock and baptism

When Yvonne Chiu was a student at Tamsui Institute of Industrial & Business Administration (now known as Aletheia University), she was also a Chinese tutor for children in an expatriate family. The father of Yvonne's student was Roy Hall, a lawyer who worked in the Military Assistance Advisory Group of the United States Armed Forces. His wife was Joyce, and the entire family were devout Christians. In order to learn more about American culture, Yvonne Chiu would go to church with the family every weekend. By immersing herself in the lives of the Hall family, Yvonne picked up Western dining etiquette and virtually became part of the family. "I even bought a Western cutlery set in order to practise at home. When my mom saw what I was doing, she exclaimed, 'You've gone nuts!'" Yvonne Chiu could not contain her smile at this memory. "Later on, I was baptized in a church. During the ceremony, I wasn't thinking of anything really, except for how cold the water was. Papa Roy said to me, 'Good for you.' Personally, I just felt that it was a cleansing ritual, but deep down I knew that God wants us to do good deeds. On another note, in the West, people are encouraged to ask questions. Whenever I had any doubts about the English language, I would not hesitate to raise questions. Sometimes I would even write essays in English for Papa Roy to critique, so that I might learn through my mistakes."

Yvonne smiled at various points during the interview as she switched between Chinese, Taiwanese, and English effortlessly. It seemed that the main reason why Yvonne was able to weave freely between local and global settings could be largely attributed to her exposure to various cultures in her youth.

When China and the United States decided to sever diplomatic ties, Roy had to return to the states with his family. Information was not readily available in those days, and every Taiwanese person was worried about a future in which they did not have the United States as an ally. Yvonne was not exempt from that sentiment, and she asked Roy, "Is Taiwan going to be in trouble?"

Roy's reassuring reply was a surprise to Yvonne, "Don't worry. Taiwan occupies an extremely important strategic position. Extremely important!"

At that time, Yvonne was still unfamiliar with the ways of the world, so she merely took Roy's words as a form of reassurance instead of understanding the wisdom behind what he said. Now, on hindsight, she was still in awe when she realized that Roy's confidence in Taiwan was not baseless, "Papa Roy knew, even 40 years ago, how important Taiwan is in relation to the rest of the world!"

Then, the Hall family returned to Alabama. "Some time later, I flew to America to catch up with them." At this point, Yvonne Chiu's clear voice took on a melancholic undertone, "Little did I expect that the second time I made this trip would be to say goodbye. Mama Joyce called me to tell me that Papa Roy has passed away…" I went to Alabama to lay down flowers at his grave, and memories of their selfless and caring nature flooded my mind. I can't thank them enough."

A group photo of Yvonne Chiu with the whole family of her foreigner father and mother and their kids

A trading company in Taiwan, a chance to see the world

In the 1960s, there was a Datong hospital beside the hair salon that Yvonne's family ran. Yvonne, who was busy day in and day out at the salon, looked up to her neighbors as inspiration. She saw that her neighbors traveled overseas frequently, and so the young Yvonne told herself, "One day, I will go overseas myself!"

Come 1976, Yvonne Chiu, who was then in her early twenties, went to the United States all by herself. At that point, she was already running a trading company in Taiwan. Due to the nature of the business, she had to go abroad to meet clients frequently, and she made a lot of foreign friends this way. The observant and inquisitive Yvonne picked up various pointers about other cultures through these friends. Yvonne once met an elderly gentleman from Oklahoma in Taiwan. She noticed that whenever he was having Western cuisine, this gentleman would order a glass of martini to go with the meal. Martini is the favorite drink of James Bond 007, and, having observed this gentleman down a few martinis, olives and all, the young Yvonne could no longer hold her curiosity in. She asked the man, "Why do you only drink martinis?" The elderly man replied, "This is the drink of choice for gentlemen in the upper class!" Since that day, the martini, with its high-class connotations, became Yvonne Chiu's drink of choice as well. She said with a smile, "I have always been this way even when I was a girl. If I see that someone was doing something that I ought to learn, I will make sure I remember it, so that I could assimilate into a foreign culture and adapt to foreign customs as quickly as possible."

During Yvonne's travels between Taiwan and the United States, she made the acquaintance of a captain from the Northwest Airlines, and also got to know his family. Every time Yvonne Chiu went to Seattle, the captain would organize gatherings and parties, and it was through these events that Yvonne got to know even more foreign friends, who later presented Yvonne Chiu with opportunities for her to make a name for herself in the United States.

The fearlessness of youth: Venturing to the United States alone

"I first stayed in Seattle for eight years. In the 70s, there weren't many chances for Americans to meet Taiwanese people, so my friends introduced me to more people. Slowly, my social circle grew." With a smile, Yvonne Chiu started singing, "My day starts before the first light of dawn, no one knows the hardships I go through⋯" Yvonne Chiu, homesick and alone in a foreign land, sang this song to herself as she set out to work every morning to give herself a little push to get through yet another day.

A young Asian girl trying to find her place in the United States, Yvonne had to stretch her dollars in every aspect. Being in the furniture business, she needed packaging materials, and they cost 5 US dollars per set! Knowing her troubles, Yvonne's friend gave her a tip: she could use the extra paper from The Seattle Times' operations for her packaging. Another friend suggested that she could get paper boxes from stationery shops. So, with the help of her friends, Yvonne got herself a van, and her company was open for business.

It was no surprise to anyone that the petite and pretty Yvonne Chiu had a couple of interesting encounters, one of which happened when she first arrived in Seattle. Yvonne asked for the bill after a meal, but the waiter told her that someone had already paid for her. This was when she realized that "it appeared that I [she] had quite a few admirers"! Also, because of her youthful looks, she was often asked if she was old enough to be drinking whenever she tried to order alcoholic drinks. In the beginning, she would proudly wave her ID card in front of the staff's eyes and say, "I am old enough to drink!" However, the same thing kept recurring and became somewhat of a bother. Yvonne returned to Seattle more than 10 years later and visited the same bar again, "I got my ID card ready, but this time, they didn't ask for it. So it seems like I've matured quite a bit over the last 10 years."

"I had long hair back then. Some people would ask me about my family, and I didn't want to tell them that I was in the US alone, so I would say that I have a twin sister. Yvonne was the one who let her hair down and handled business negotiations, and Yvonny was my twin who wore her hair in a ponytail and handled the operations." Yvonne smiled, amused, "I didn't expect that my clients bought the story about my twin sister. No one ever figured out that it I made it up! On another note, many of my friends told me that the market in Texas was more considerable, so I went to Texas for a week to check out the city. True enough, I saw a wider market, so I started networking with potential partners in Texas."

Before she went to Texas, Yvonne thought of the United States as modern, cultured, and stylish. Texas, however, shattered that impression. Yvonne recounted her experience of being gawked at openly in the more rural areas of Texas, "Americans living in that part of the country had never seen Asians, especially not someone like me, an Asian woman with a full face of makeup. I asked my friend why everyone was looking at me, and my friend told me laughingly, 'These Texans think that you're an alien!'"

Remaining calm in the face of danger: Saying "no" to a Mexican drug lord

Being all alone in a foreign land, Yvonne Chiu was extremely mindful of her personal safety, and so she developed many ways to protect herself. For instance, she would turn down her clients' dinner invitations; when she stayed in motels, she would book the room closest to the reception counter, so that the staff would be able to hear her cries for help should an emergency arise; she always returned to her room before sunset and did not step out until the next morning (a result of this "safety measure" was that Yvonne got really good at doing her nails); if she left her seat during a meal, she would not drink from the same glass when she got back. However, for all her precautions, she could not foresee what fate had in store for her.

Once, Yvonne Chiu had a business meeting with a Mexican businessman who ran a furniture factory to discuss the possibility of her being his agent. The ever-cautious Yvonne had a friend from college who had been in Los Angeles for years drive her to the meeting. The meeting went way more smoothly than Yvonne expected, and the Mexican businessman extended a lunch invitation to her, "I don't suppose you've had lunch yet! Let me buy you a meal." It was noon, and Yvonne was indeed hungry after a morning's work, so she agreed to the meal, all the while thinking that the Mexican man was exceedingly generous, for he not only agreed to all her business pitches, and even offered to give her a treat.

After lunch, the Mexican man did not drive Yvonne back to the factory; instead, he took her to a mansion. The two-story mansion was built in an M shape. Before the mansion, more than 10 expensive cars were parked neatly in a row. The mansion had rooms that reminded one of luxury hotels. Chandeliers cast dreamy lights and shadows in various rooms, and each of these rooms was designed differently, with exotic furnishings and rare crystals promising endless

splendor and opulence! It was just like the movies! "You may stay here," the Mexican looked at Yvonne, "If you wish to go anywhere, you may have your pick of the cars!" Why, it seemed like the martinis that Yvonne drank were taking effect, and she was turning into a Bond girl!

The two of them returned to the Mexican man's office, where he took a call. Yvonne caught snippets of the conversation and heard several mentions of the word "powder". It dawned on her, "Could it be⋯ that this man also deals in drugs, on top of his furniture business? Maybe he was hiding drugs in the furniture!" Yvonne was at a loss for what to do. Should she walk away? Should she get out as quickly as possible? Various options ran through her head, but she told herself that she had to stay calm and keep her guard up!

It was the 1980s, and mobile phones were not common in those times. Inspiration struck, and she asked to borrow the phone under the pretense of having to make plans with a friend. She called her friend from university, whom she had discussed contingency plans with earlier, and asked her to come immediately. As soon as her friend arrived, Yvonne hopped onto the car and got out of there without even saying "goodbye" to the Mexican man.

Saying "no" in the face of such temptations in a perilous setting reminiscent of a James Bond movie – this is indeed something that only Yvonne Chiu, more extraordinary and twice as stunning as a Bond girl, can do!

Linda Reisman, twin sister from another country

After telling the exciting story, Yvonne recomposed herself and regained her usual serenity. "Later on, I moved to Texas. Linda Reisman, who lived in Denver, took really great care of me. She saw that I was a young girl running my own business in Denver, so she invited me to stay at her place and even lent me her car. Her father was a Jewish American, but she always said that I was her twin sister whom her father dropped accidentally from the airplane when he was flying to the United States." With the tension dissipated, Yvonne's candid laughter filled the room once more. "Linda's folks were very kind and treated me as part of their family, and we grew really close. Linda was a good cook, and I made my signature spring rolls and dumplings for her family in return for their hospitality. Besides the sharing of good food, it was also a chance for me to share the 'gastronomic culture' of Taiwan!"

Yvonne Chiu and Linda Reisman's family

Making a living in Texas

"Working as a furniture agent in Texas, I made my first pot of gold and got a Mercedes Benz500 as a reward for myself! I got myself a green one. Mobile phones had just started appearing in the market, and I carried my chunky mobile phone and washed my car all by myself at the car wash, in a fur coat no less! I was very proud of myself, for I could afford all this because of my hard work!"

Yvonne Chiu had every right to be proud of herself. She once received a huge order that had to be shipped out before Christmas, but the rules were that new orders could only come in by the end of October, because if orders came in later than that, the factories had to work overtime to meet the deadline. In other words, the factory owner would decline this order even if the order slip were sent directly to him. Yvonne Chiu was understandably anxious, but she still remained calm enough to come up with a novel solution. She wrote the word "Lush" in huge letters on the order slip that she had to fax to the factory, and received a call from the factory owner shortly, "What does 'lush' mean?" He was perplexed.

"That was the call I was waiting for!" Yvonne Chiu explained her ploy with a smile, "I knew that if I had spelt 'rush' correctly, my order slip would not have stood out among all the order slips from the various agents, and the factory owner would not have paid attention to my request. However, if I wrote 'lush', he would call me out of curiosity, and so I could take the chance to put in my request to ensure that my shipment could be made before the deadline."

Yvonne's competitive nature led her to develop numerous solutions to realize her goals. She went to the United States as a budding entrepreneur and went on to become a successful businesswoman, increasing her worth exponentially. It is also her fearless nature that led her through experiences that made her the

extraordinary woman that she is today. The combination of her being born and raised in a Hakka family and her assimilation into American society resulted in the birth of her unique softpower! Yvonne Chiu stated that she understood that the only way she could go was forward, "When I was abroad, I lived each day positively, because I knew that I didn't have the right to be negative!"

Chapter Three

Transforming Lives
through education

Full sponsorship for impoverished children
Bringing back international gold awards

Paying it forward

Environment and circumstances have a huge impact on people in their formative years. Children growing up in less fortunate situations often have to fight an uphill battle to overcome their circumstances. What is the reason behind the petite Yvonne Chiu's motivation to sponsor less fortunate young people to go overseas for competitions, year after year without fail?

"I came back to Taiwan many times when I was working in America, and Taiwan has never failed to warm my heart each and every time I returned." Yvonne Chiu hugged her chest and leaned back gently on the couch, "Every time I missed home, I would sing 'My homeland, at dusk'⋯ "With her eyes softly closed, longing seeped into Yvonne Chiu's voice shortly into the song. She choked up, and her voice took on a nasal quality, "I'm reminded of how my father always emphasized that we ought to pay it forward after we become more financially well-off."

A lady entrepreneur back in her hometown, a success story in the early 1990s – the next phase of Yvonne Chiu's life, when she got acquainted with the IT world, was just about to begin!

● Typhoon Herbfund-raising concert

Mega-typhoon Herb struck Taiwan in 1996 and wreaked havoc across Taiwan. Many places in Taipei experienced major floods, and Taiwan suffered economic losses of more than 30 billion New Taiwan Dollars! As the Director of Xizhi Education Association, Yvonne Chiu spared no effort in expediting the rebuilding of schools affected by the disasters. Yvonne Chiu invited the musician Chien Wen-hsiu, Japanese pianist Anna Azusa Fujita, who was in Taiwan at that

time, and vocalist Lily Lu to come together for a fund-raising concert. Proceeds from the sale of the tickets and 50 computers from the Institute for Information Industry all went to schools in Xizhi in need of these resources. Ever humble, Yvonne Chiu said that she stepped forward only because she wanted to encourage more people to help those in need, and the resulting heightened awareness that members of the public cultivated towards disaster-relief and education support was a happy byproduct of her effort.

Yvonne Chiu organized a fund-raising concert for schools in Xizhi that are impacted by Typhoon Herb (Musician Chien Wen-hsiu on the left)

From the neighborhood to the nation:
Organizing the National Computer Art Competition

The rebuilding of schools in Xizhi presented a great chance for the schools to upgrade their computer equipment and laboratories. "I thought of how computer technology took off in the United States, and I realized that this is exactly what Taiwan needed! Hence, a thought materialized in my mind: I want to give less fortunate children in Taiwan a chance to turn their lives around. Since Taiwan was in need of computer-savvy professionals, why not train these children in terms of computer literacy? This way, not only could I provide education and skills training, and subsequently open new doors for these children, I could also play a part in contributing to Taiwan's growth!" That was also the time when the 486 CPU was released. Yvonne Chiu recalled, "I worked with the then-town mayor of XizhiChou Ya-shu, Deputy Director of the Computer Center of the Ministry of Education Liu Chin-ho, as well as BerrySoft[3] to organize a Children's Computer Art Competition every Saturday. It was the first such competition in Taiwan, and even the Ministry of Education was impressed by our initiative."

"I created an environment that is competitive yet friendly, in order to motivate the children to learn. Once they experience the joy of success, their enthusiasm for learning will naturally increase. When more people start to pick up computer skills, this learning culture will then become an integral part of society."

---

[3] BerrySoft was founded in July 1992 and became formally known as Strawberry Software Inc. in April 2000. BerrySoft designs a variety of learning materials catered to the needs of learners of various ages. With the aid of digital tools, school children, parents, and teachers can all pick up computer skills at BerrySoft.

Yvonne Chiu organized the Young Computer Artist Competition in Xizhi in order to promote a culture of computer literacy.

Connecting with the world: Boosting computer education in Taiwan

When it comes to the achievements of these young ladies and gentlemen, Yvonne Chiu could not help beaming with pride! "I adopted a bottom-up approach when it came to promoting computer literacy in Taiwan. Once the children's computer literacy reaches a level comparable to international standards, it sets the foundation for them to advance to international platforms. This way, our children will be able to connect with the world in terms of their computer literacy skills!" Yvonne Chiu said with conviction, "To level the digital playing field, we had to start building up our nation's computer literacy. No detail was too small to take care of!"

Yvonne Chiu exuded a sense of motherly love and exhibited the vision of an entrepreneur at the same time. She said, "I created a platform for the children to showcase their talents. We then went from local competitions to international ones, and the team grew stronger and bonded in the process. I told them, 'If you keep working hard, international prizes are not out of your reach!'" Yvonne Chiu started this computer educationjourney from the town of Xizhi by first systematically pushing for the training of teachers for computer education, before eventually finding a spot for Taiwan youths on the world stage!

● Worldwide Competition on Microsoft Office

At the beginning of the 21st century, Yvonne Chiu ran into a friend from America who told her that Microsoft was pushing for specialist training for Microsoft Office. By then, Yvonne Chiu had been working in the field of computer education for years. So, when she learnt about this, she realized that Microsoft's direction matched her understanding of worldwide trends in computer education. Hence, she set up Elite IT Pte. Ltd. and became the

2000 was the year that Taiwan took part in the Worldwide Competition on Microsoft Office for the first time. Yvonne Chiu and her protégés with then-Vice President of Taiwan Annette Lu (second from left).

general agent in Taiwan for Microsoft Office Specialist (MOS) courses. MOS is the only international profession certification course recognized by Microsoft itself. This course is available in 27 languages and 153 countries and regions around the world. Yvonne Chiu visited numerous vocational schools, tertiary institutions, and tuition centers personally to coach students on the certification requirements. The certification, once attained, transforms these young students into internationally accredited professionals!

In order to connect Taiwan with the world, Yvonne Chiu organized a national competition every year in May. Through the competition, she selected outstanding participants and sent them overseas for the international competition. For its 8th installation in 2008, the local preliminaries for the Worldwide Competition on Microsoft Office were divided by region for the first time. Contestants had to compete against their peers in the regional rounds first, held respectively in

northern Taiwan, central Taiwan, and southern Taiwan, before making it to the national competition. In the same year, Yvonne Chiu, who brought the MOS certification course to Taiwan, said in her speech, "To level the digital playing field, we have to start building up our nation's computer literacy. No area is overlooked, and no child left behind!" The real value of these competitions was in allowing Taiwanese young people to gain international exposure through their outstanding computer skills. As they participated at the international level, they got to meet and interact with national champions from all over the world. Friendships forged will translate to a broadened horizon. Hence, not only did Yvonne Chiu aspire to be Taiwan's version of Bill Gates, she also hoped that the student participants would also have similar aspirations!

Over the last 17 years, in line with her goal of grooming internationally accredited IT professionals, Yvonne Chiu has helped more than 700 thousand students in Taiwan acquire international computer certifications. Yvonne Chiu became part of the IT industry in a twist of fate, and she has fully devoted herself to this new career trajectory and brought about positive changes to the local computer education scene. Even though Yvonne Chiu was not trained in related fields, she knew that her effort over the past 17 years had produced a strong pool of Taiwanese IT professionals, who would have the capability to meet the challenges of waves of technological advancements head-on and open even more doors for Taiwan in the grand scheme of things.

In 2008, due to the overwhelming number of participants, the preliminary rounds for the MOS competition were held in 3 regions in Taiwan, namely northern Taiwan, central Taiwan, and southern Taiwan. This was the first time that such an arrangement had to be made, and it is a testament of the effectiveness of Yvonne Chiu's promotion of computer education across the nation.

● Full sponsorships for financially disadvantaged students

Yvonne Chiu remembered her own impoverished childhood when her family had to take loans from relatives to pay her school fees. The experience left a mark on Yvonne. Hence, decades later, she developed a soft spot for children from poor families, becoming a mother-like figure to them. She has helped countless students from financially disadvantaged families to attain their MOS certification. "They don't have to prove to me that they are from low-income families. I'll help them as long as they have been nominated by their teachers or professors," she said, gently and kindly, "Doing charity work is never a bad thing, but we have to be mindful of hurting the children's feelings."

9 world championships in 7 consecutive years

Before 2008, the MOS and ACA World Championships only involved the used of Word and Excel. However, the worldly Yvonne Chiu has already gotten a grasp on the direction that the world was moving towards, and she shared her thoughts with the organizers of the competition.

"I told the organizers that everybody needed to know how to do presentations in today's world. It is an important and useful skill not just in school, but also in the workplace, when people have to do presentations during interviews, product launches, as well as pitches and proposals. Thus, they ought to include a PowerPoint segment in this competition."

In 2009, more than 80 thousand participants from 53 countries around the world took part in the competition. The number of participants was a record high, and these teams made it to the finals after rounds of competitions at the district, national, and regional levels. Taiwan emerged as one of the teams to make it to the grand championship round held in Toronto, Canada, and the team brought home the championship title in world championships for the first time! On that day, Yvonne Chiu shed tears of joy. All her hard work has paid off, and she could finally enjoy the fruits of her success. The team did Taiwan proud, and their victory was widely covered in various papers and media channels. For the next 7 years, Yvonne Chiu continued to groom new talents personally, and won 9 world championships for Taiwan!

In 2009, Taiwan brought home the championship title in the MOS and ACA World Championships for the first time!

We are from Taiwan. Not China!

The following year, Yvonne Chiu led a team to take part in the competition in Utah, the United States, and the Taiwanese team did Taiwan proud again by emerging as the world champion in not one, but two categories! However, during the award presentation ceremony that afternoon, the emcee announced that the team was "from China" instead of "from Taiwan". Upon hearing that, Yvonne Chiu voiced her strong disapproval, "We are from Taiwan. Not China!" She then made the emcee say "from Taiwan" thrice, in order to get the message across. Her forthright outburst gave the governor sitting by the side a shock!

Yvonne Chiu arrived at the venue of the evening session of the award ceremony early, and was greeted by a question from her partner from the MOS certification team, "Yvonne, what can I do?" The question came out of the blue, and Yvonne Chiu was perplexed, so she returned the question, "What?"

It turned out that someone requested that the Taiwanese flag be changed to one that said "Chinese Taipei". The ever-straightforward Yvonne Chiu, whose business dealings with the organization were up to a million US dollars in value, asked her MOS partner plainly, "Do you want my business or not?" Her business partner was at a loss, "I want your business, but I don't know what to do. They want to change your flag. Tell me what to do!"

All the flags were to be projected onto the big screen at the venue, and the image file for the Taiwanese flag was already deleted and could not be retrieved. "Give me a few seconds!" Yvonne Chiu asked for some time and racked her brain for a solution. Just then, inspiration struck, and she had her answer! "Delete all the flags and don't show any!"

It was a spark of genius, and the MOS representative agreed that that was the best possible solution, "That I can do." So, within seconds, Yvonne Chiu came up with the perfect solution and arrived at a win-win situation. She resisted political pressure from the international community and achieved a homerun for Taiwan.

Inner peace stems from compassion

The President of Uruguay, known as the poorest president in the world, once said that love for the world brings calm to one's heart. Speaking about her sponsorship of students from humble backgrounds in their quest to achieve world championship titles, Yvonne Chiu smiled and said, "What I did was to give Taiwanese young people a chance to rub shoulders and compete with world-class participants from all around the world, and at the same time bring back trophies for Taiwan. What could possibly be more rewarding than this?"

● Politician joined the students in addressing Yvonne Chiu as "Mama Chiu"

Before the competition, Yvonne Chiu would always practice international etiquette and English with the students, so that they can put their best foot forward when they are overseas. "After all, every time we step beyond our shores, we become ambassadors of Taiwan." To allow the students to concentrate on the competition without worrying about the situation back home, Yvonne Chiu applied for funding from the Ministry of Foreign Affairs. With her help, each participant can now receive NT10,000 for taking part in the competition! Coincidentally, the MOS competition always takes place around Mother's Day, so the students took to calling Yvonne Chiu "Mama Chiu".

Chen Ou-po, a member of the Legislative Yuan who was part of the Ministry of Foreign Affairs and National Defence, was from Yilan. When he presented the Taiwanese flag to Yvonne Chiu, he said to her, "If our students from Yilan become world champions, I will join the kids in calling you 'Mama Chiu'!" During the competition, Chen Ou-po asked Yvonne Chiu privately about her motivation to groom the younger generation. To that, Yvonne Chiu answered, "To level the digital playing field, so that Taiwan can connect with the rest

of the world, and so that our young people are able to compete with their counterparts from other countries in 10 or 20 years!" True enough, the students from Yilan did Mama Chiu proud in that year's competition and won the championship! At the press conference held to share the achievements of the team, Chen Ou-po walked in and immediately called out, loud and clear, "Good day, Mama Chiu!"

Yvonne Chiu encouraged the Taiwanese representatives to actively interact with their counterparts from other countries. These young participants would go on to become the next generation of IT professionals in Taiwan and inject new energy into the industry!

● With a flag on their back, they are set to conquer new grounds

"Every time we set off for a competition, the students would take the initiative to display the Taiwanese flag on their backpacks, as if they were going onto a battlefield and fighting for their homeland." Yvonne Chiu was very moved by their action. "It's quite strange. No one taught the students to do that, but they all did. Also, whenever they got an award, they would take a big flag out of their backpack the way magicians would pull things out of thin air in a performance. The children would show off the flag and take photographs with it; some would even kiss the flag and wear it around their shoulders as they cheered and jumped in excitement." At this memory, Yvonne Chiu wiped off the tears welling up in her eyes. She was so proud, and so moved. In her eyes was the future of Taiwan,dazzling the crowd on an international stage. The triumphant spotlight belonged not only to the winners, but also to each and every Taiwanese citizen.

Every time a participant wins an award in an international competition, the team would hold up the Taiwanese flag proudly and announce to the world, "We are from Taiwan!"

Chapter Four

The Mother of Cybersecurity

Sparing no effort in legislating cybersecurity

The Mother of Cybersecurity: A bridge between hackers and the government

In her dealings with her foreign counterparts, Yvonne Chiu observed that the issue of information security and privacy would often come up in international conferences. Thus, she began to learn about what cybersecurity entails. During her computer education advocacy work, she got to know young hackers from Taiwan. In the early days, hacker conventions in Taiwan were organized by young people with a passion for hacking. Whenever these young hackers came to Mama Chiu for help, they would always get it, for Yvonne Chiu has always been a staunch supporter of computer education. She would also take the chance to remind them to be White Hat ethical hackers who defeat their criminal counterpart, the Black Hat crackers, the latter being people who wanted nothing but to wreak havoc in the cyber world.

Yvonne Chiu spoke at the Hacks in Taiwan Conference (HITCON) one particular year. She has been involved in activities related to cybersecurity for years by then, and has herself been keenly aware of global trends. She put forth the idea that Taiwan should strive to become a "Security Island" with world-class software experts, who could form a think tank to provide assistance to other countries in the area of cybersecurity. Her idea gained traction, so much so that high-ranking officials working with the President asked for Yvonne Chiu's help to invite hackers to the President's office for a dialogue session.

Speaking of the hackers, Yvonne Chiu smiled fondly, "They go by handles and nicknames instead of their real names. These young people don't use name cards, even when meeting government officials!" That being said, in her interactions with the hackers, one could repeatedly hear them calling her "Mama Chiu" affectionately and loudly. It suffices to say that Yvonne Chiu is the true Mother of Cybersecurity in Taiwan in the hearts of these young people!

Yvonne Chiu and the young hackers. She encourages them to become White Hat ethical hackers whose job is to defeat malicious Black Hat crackers.

● *Information Security*: A partner in promoting cybersecurity

Information Security is the first magazine in Taiwan to focus on the issue of information security, as per its namesake. Chancing upon the magazine, Yvonne Chiu was pleasantly surprised, "I realized that there are other people like me in Taiwan who are working on promoting cybersecurity!" Yvonne Chiu went on to become fast friends with Shi Jia-hua, who was in charge of *Information Security*. Shi Jia-huashared enthusiastically, "Even before we started this magazine, there was already a group of people working on this issue in Taiwan. After we launched our publication, people concerned about the issue of cybersecurity naturally gravitated towards us and shared their thoughts and opinions with us." Identity verification has already received a lot of attention in places like South Korea, Singapore, and even China at that point in time. It was a forward-looking measure, but at that time, Taiwan had yet to set up a legal body to look into the issue; all Taiwan had was just an annual cybersecurity report. Shi Jia-hua said in all seriousness, "It was only after I started to delve into the matter of cybersecurity that I realized that there were cyber-armies who had free access to confidential files in the government database. This was something that the masses were not aware of. Information breach was not just a security issue for businesses; it could have a huge impact on social stability and national security!"

Inviting an FBI agent to speak in Taiwan

In those days, most people had no awareness of cybersecurity. In order to educate the public, Yvonne Chiu invited IT experts from other countries to conduct talks in Taiwan, one of which was an FBI cybersecurity agent. As for herself, Yvonne Chiu explained the concept of cybersecurity to business owners of listed companies in layman's terms, "The database of a company is like a house, which could sometimes be invaded by 'invisible foes' such as water leakage and tree branches growing into the house. These invaders are referred to as 'hackers' in the cyber-world. To prevent their attacks, we have to have pre-emptive measures in place!"

Since 2007, Yvonne Chiu has invited experts to write monthly articles pertaining to the issue of cybersecurity, but such essays could be very dry for the average reader. Shi Jia-hua poked fun at his own field of expertise, "Trying to understand an article on cybersecurity would be, to most people, as difficult as comprehending an essay written in archaic Chinese. However, Yvonne Chiu came up with a simple way to help the layman understand our discussions." Yvonne Chiu smiled, "We summarized the content of an article into four-frame comics so that it's easier to understand." Hence, every such article came with an interesting and fun comic, and this column has become an important serialized feature in Information Security. Shi Jia-hua affirmed the move, for he saw the impact of their effort to educate the masses on cybersecurity. As more and more people learn about cybersecurity, the industry matured at a rapid rate. The credit goes to the insightful Yvonne Chiu!

Yvonne Chiu invited an FBI IT expert to talk about the importance of information security at the China University of Technology in Taiwan.

● Push for legislation: Press conference at the Legislative Yuan

The Personal Information Protection Act was passed in Taiwan's Legislative Yuan in April 2010 after years of hard work, time, and effort by committed individuals. However, to Yvonne Chiu, the Act still left much to be desired, "even though it was already a huge step forward for Taiwan!" Ho Chuan-te, the current Secretary-General of the National Development Council, who was keenly aware of the pivotal role that Yvonne Chiu played in pushing for the Personal Information Protection Act, as well as her contributions to the field of information security in Taiwan, said to her, "Mama Chiu, aren't you something!" Despite their success, Yvonne Chiu and Shi Jia-hua knew that Taiwan still had a long way to go in terms of its cybersecurity practices.

Reality versus dreams: Story of an aspiring hacker

Back then, professional know-hows about information security did nothing to increase an IT professional's income. Hence, many professionals in the industry stayed on in the field for passion more than anything else. However, their passion could only do so much for them if they did not receive an income proportionate to their skills and dedication. Once, a well-known and accomplished hacker said to Shi Jia-hua, "I am going to get married soon, so I might not be able to continue training as a hacker." Shi Jia-hua felt really sorry for that hacker, for being a professional hacker was his lifelong dream, but he had to let it go due to his responsibility to his family. When reality shatters dreams, and the two diverge, it tells us that there was something wrong with Taiwan's IT industry, and something should be considered about it!

Yvonne Chiu shared that she allowed that hacker to use part of her office to set up his own business, and she even introduced a lot of clients to him. Once, the National Development Council went with them to attend a conference in Las Vegas, and the council representative expressed that they did not have a high budget. Yvonne Chiu did not hesitate in her reply, "Not a problem. I'll help!"

"It is not difficult to attract young talents. You just need to make sure they get one of two things — a sense of accomplishment, or a good salary." Shi Jia-hua, who stayed on in the cybersecurity business for his passion, said with a sigh, "Taiwan's professional training industry has become mature, but the employment market is still lacking in an awareness of cybersecurity issues. People in other countries know that cybersecurity measures are a form of risk aversion that would protect them from external threats, but Taiwanese people don't see it that way because they do not see the importance of cybersecurity measures. Technical experts are everywhere in the cyber-world, but who can help us when a company's information security is threatened? How can we solve the problem? How can we resolve the issue? Hence, the way I see it, Taiwan needed a revolutionary change in the way we approach the issue of cybersecurity."

Being a god-sent investor to Armorize

In 2013, Armorize was acquired by Proofpoint, a listed email encryption company in the United States, for 25 million US dollars (about 750 million NT dollars). It set the record for the highest price at which a Taiwanese software company was acquired by another company. However, not many are aware of Armorize's story before it became one of the hottest newcomers in the industry.

Back in the day, government webpages in Taiwan were often the targets of Mainland China's cyber-attacks. Chinese hackers would insert malicious codes into these websites, so that anyone who visited the sites would be infected with a computer virus. In 2005, the founder of Armorize saw the pressing need for Taiwan to enhance its cybersecurity measures, so he started his own company to work towards this goal. However, in Taiwan, challenges facing IT startups were many, what's more a startup in the cybersecurity field! Knowing that Mama Chiu has always been an advocate of cybersecurity, Armorize founder Wayne Huang approached her and proposed a mutual investment. Yvonne Chiu, who knew all too well the importance of cybersecurity, agreed to Wayne Huang's proposal without a moment's hesitation. Thus, Yvonne Chiu became the angel that Amorize needed in the early days of its establishment.

Armorize lived up to its promise and grew to become one of the leading local companies in the cybersecurity field within just a matter of years. Even major foreign companies recognized its achievements. Armorize's success was the best testament to Yvonne Chiu's vision, that Taiwan has the capacity to become a "Security Island" and a cybersecurity think tank for other countries!

Digital Prowess as National Prowess, cybersecurity as National Security

After she was sworn in, President Tsai Ing-wen came up with the slogan "Digital Prowess as National Prowess, Cybersecurity as National Security" Yvonne Chiu shared, "That was the theme of the Computer Software and Service Industry Development Proposal that CISA came up with before the 2015 presidential election." Yvonne Chiu invited presidential candidate Tsai Ing-wen to the event, "I said to them that we need to have a change in mindset and also push for innovation." Due to Yvonne Chiu's strong advocacy of the issue of cybersecurity, Tsai Ing-wen set out to boost national defence technology after she became President, and Yvonne Chiu was the only representative from the private sector on the President's panel of advisors.

● Creating a whole industry, then retreating into the background

The far-sighted Yvonne Chiu predicted that cybersecurity was bound to become a staple in the global IT industry in future. So, she founded the Taiwan Privacy Consultants Association (TWPCA) in 2007 and invited ChenJenn-Nan, General Manager of an e-commerce website, to be theChairman. She personally headed the Taiwan Personal Data Protection Association (TWPDA) and, working with *Information Security*, brought about greater awareness to the issue of cybersecurity! "We virtually created the cybersecurity industry in Taiwan!" Yvonne Chiu said with pride, "If we hadn't worked together to get more people talking about these issues back then, perhaps Taiwan would still be lagging behind in terms of cybersecurity even now! The cybersecurity industry gained attention of the general public because I was relentless in my advocacy!"

Yvonne Chiu also put forth the suggestion of grooming Certified Ethical Hackers (CEH)[4] to Ho Chuan-te, who was the Director of the Department of Information Management in the Research, Development and Evaluation

Commission of the Executive Yuan back then, and is now the Secretary-General of the National Development Council. After her work with Shi Jia-hua to push for legislation on cybersecurity was done, Yvonne Chiu chose to take a step back and allowed a more suitable candidate to take over on the frontline, as she felt that her mission has concluded. However, Yvonne Chiu has never stopped working to better Taiwan's IT industry!

[4] The CEH certification course introduces students to common tools and methods employed by malicious hackers, so that the students can get an idea of how hackers work and think. From here, they would have a stronger understanding of how to enhance online security and better protect computer systems from cyber-attacks, as well as how to guard against system breaches by unlawful hackers. "Ethical hackers" refer to hackers whose actions do not violate ethical guidelines. As such, CEH certification is also referred to as "White Hat certification" in order to set ethical hackers apart from unlawful and unethical crackers.

Chapter Five

A social butterfly
with a gentle soul

Meeting with the Dalai Lama on his Journey of Compassion and Wisdom

"Seldom will I fail to achieve something I set my mind on," Yvonne Chiu proclaimed with pride, "I will brainstorm for all possible solutions to overcome any challenges that come my way!" The extraordinarily strong-willed Yvonne Chiu said, "If you lack the guts to grab life by the horns, you will not achieve anything even if all the stars aligned." Her determination and iron will never wavering, Yvonne Chiu accomplished numerous tasks that many would see as "mission(s) impossible".

Towards the end of March 2001, the Dalai Lama visited Taiwan on his 10-day *Journey of Compassion and Wisdom*. The Dalai Lama had said that the only woman whom he would meet had to be one who was "very important", so everybody thought that Annette Lu Hsiu-lien, the Vice President then, would be the one. At a time when no other woman had the privilege of meeting the Dalai Lama in person, Yvonne Chiu reached out to all her contacts for help. Eventually, Yvonne Chiu got the chance to take a picture with the Dalai Lama before he gave a speech, thanks to a special arrangement made by a friend of hers.

Yvonne Chiu and the Dalai Lama

Rotary Club Group Study Exchange

Yvonne Chiu has a wealth of experience behind her. She was a consultant for the Executive Yuan, the Managing Director for the Institute for Information Industry, and a consultant for an orchestra. Her career was truly astonishing, spanning disparate industries and fields, from politics to IT, and even to arts and culture. When asked about the work that left the deepest impression and most long-lasting influence on her, Yvonne Chiu's answer, once again, set her apart from most people, who would probably answer with an encounter with certain leaders and consultants of established organizations.

This was Yvonne Chiu's answer, "The Rotary Club Group Study Exchange (GSE)."

The former Director of Medicare for Region 3480 of the Rotary Club, who had served the club for more than 30 years and groomed numerous young talents, explained what GSE is:

"In 1965, the Rotary Foundation organized GSE programs for young professionals in more than 530 places around the world. During the exchange program, the participants would get a chance to go on an overseas trip. Because everyone on the trip is a working professional, they could schedule visits to organizations related to their own area of work, on top of experiencing a different way of life."

The Medicare Director produced Yvonne Chiu's old name card as he told the story, "She was a really responsible and competent tour leader. The current Chairperson of Radio Taiwan International was part of her GSE group. I met her for the first time at the Charter Ceremony of the Rotary Club of Taipei Fu-Jung and found out that she was one of the founding members of the club, and she acted as the secretary in its early days. I thought to myself, there was definitely something in her that stood out. If not, she would not have been elected as secretary in such a big women's group!"

The GSE is a recurring event organized by the Rotary Club to allow its members to visit different countries in the spirit of cultural exchange and learning. In 2001, Yvonne Chiu led a group of Rotary Club members on a trip to Georgia, USA. During the 35-day trip, the group visited the homes of Rotary Club members in Georgia, and their mission was to share about Taiwan within a short time and let their hosts learn more about Taiwanese culture. It was an important task, and every member of the group was anxious about doing a good job. They took this cultural exchange as both the first and last one of their lives, and wanted to give it their all! Yvonne Chiu had to speak at the various district Rotary Club clubhouses that their hosts were members of, and the content of the speeches was all only decided the night before in a brainstorming session. Sometimes, on the following day, Yvonne Chiu had to speak to a 400 or 500-strong audience. She smiled at the memory and said that when she ascended the stage, she would sometimes be so nervous that her heart almost jumped out of her mouth!

Yvonne Chiu and GSE members in Georgia, the United States, on a GSE cultural immersion trip.

Despite the packed itinerary of the GSE trip, it was a fruitful trip for Yvonne Chiu. "I put in a lot of time and effort pouring over class materials and paid a lot of attention during the lessons to learn how they do certain things in the United States. I also visited a local college, Kennesaw State University, and attended the Possible Woman Leadership Conference with the university's president Dr. Betty Siegel. I had the chance to interact with outstanding women from all over the world, and learnt a lot from them in the process. The event was covered by a local paper." Yvonne Chiu took out the photograph she took at the event as well as a copy of the media report. "In 2002, I led a group of students to the USA for a competition, and specially chartered a car to bring them to all the way to Georgia to share my experiences with them. When we were there, we raninto a Rotary Club member whom I got acquainted with during the previous year during the GSE trip! He was quite surprised and asked me, 'Yvonne, why you are here!' Good friends make us feel at home anywhere in the world indeed!"

Betty Siegel is a renowned educator in Georgia, USA. She was one of the three key speakers at the 2001Possible Woman Leadership Conference (first from left).

Principal of Kennesaw State University, renowned educatorBetty Siegel, to discuss their respective education philosophy.

An unforgettable encounter with President Carter

Georgia is the home of former US President Jimmy Carter, and the GSE group had the privilege of listening to Carter speak in a church during their trip. This was a rare opportunity in itself, and what made it even more memorable was an interesting anecdote that happened during the event.

"I have been to the country of each one of you seated here, have I not?" Carter asked his audience with confidence.

"No!" Yvonne Chiu, leader of the group, answered loudly and clearly. Everyone in the church turned to look at her, curious about the lady who spoke so bluntly to a former US President.

"Where are you from?" How dare someone reply in the negative so blatantly! Carter cast a questioning look at Yvonne Chiu.

"I am from Taiwan!" Yvonne Chiu replied breezily and confidently.

Upon hearing the word "Taiwan", Carter remained silent for a moment, before confirming Yvonne Chiu's guess with a low "yes".

Carter began speaking proper. He was canvassing for funds for a Non-Governmental Organization (NGO). When he asked the crowd if anyone was willing to donate to the cause, Yvonne Chiu's arm shot up without any hesitation, "Yes, Taiwan can!"

Once again, to the astonishment of everyone who was present, Yvonne Chiu claimed another victory for Taiwan!

After his speech, Carter took a group picture with the GSE members, and their trip came to a wonderful close. Even today, this story of Yvonne Chiu's interactions with Carter is a favorite topic among those who were on that trip!

The easy grace and elegance that Yvonne Chiu exuded when she was in the United States for GSE in 2001 left a deep impression on former US President Carter.

● Reflection: One should not judge a book by itscover

Yvonne Chiu said that she was learning new things every day during the trip and getting culture shocks all the time. "There was once, we were at the car park of a supermarket with our host families, and one of our members was about to leave with a tall black guy. I was quite worried about him, so I told him that it was okay for him to turn down the invitation." At this point, Yvonne Chiu's eyes widened in vexation, "I did not expect that that man was the Vice President of a bank!" Yvonne Chiu let out a long sigh, "I did some reflection after the incident and told myself to get rid of all prejudices and stereotypes. I was wrong to have judgedhim based on the color of his skin."

Deeply committed to her responsibilities: The only re-elected GSE leader

"Yvonne Chiu was a responsible and competent GSE leader in 2001. It was no secret that she was charismatic in her bearing, diligent in facilitating cross-cultural understanding, and caring towards the group members under her charge. Thus, we nominated her as the leader for the second time, this time for a GSE trip to Alabama, USA." The Medicare Director affirmed Yvonne Chiu's commitment and enthusiasm towards the GSE program, saying that she was an exemplar of great cultural exchange practices and international diplomacy.

Yvonne Chiu has always been a staunch supporter of activities organized by the Rotary Club. During the GSE trip, she paid a visit to Mama Joyce in Alabama and the two reminisced about the good old days. Yvonne Chiu humbly said that she owed her public speaking skills to the Medicare director, for if he had not nominated her as the GSE leader twice, she would not have had the chance to prepare presentations within such short times every day. This intensive training gave her the experience she needed for her subsequent speeches at international events.

Yvonne Chiu said cheerfully that she never failed to show off her picture taken with the Dalai Lama at each GSE presentation. That photograph would always elicit envious, and even jealous, waves of "wow" from the audience. It was only then that the GSE members realized that that was the true reason why Yvonne Chiu wanted to meet the Dalai Lama! Yvonne Chiu was unreserved in sharing her tactic, "To put it bluntly, this is a tactic I employ. When you are making a presentation at an international event, you have to 'wow' t hem first. If you didn't, how would you then get their attention and leave a deep impression on them?"

An insistence on doing good

Yvonne Chiu's footsteps in practicing charity can be seen around the The nature The nature of Yvonne Chiu's charity work shares a similarity to the profile of WITSA members — both are all over the world. Yvonne Chiu said humbly that her empathy was a result of her impoverished childhood. Her parents taught her the joy of sharing, and their family often extended a helping hand to the less fortunate. "When I was a girl, I would often see my father buying entire baskets of produce from vegetables sellers from the rural areas, just so that they could call it a day sooner."

Her parents' teachings left a deep impact on Yvonne Chiu. Even now, she would often buy lots of vegetables at one go and share the greens with her family and friends. Her husband frequently teased her by asking her if she was preparing a lavish banquet for hundreds of guests. For Yvonne Chiu, her parents' teachings would often ring in her mind, "You can't live without money, but money isn't the most important thing in the world. When you have the means, you ought to give back to society and help the less fortunate."

Yvonne Chiu's character is shaped by both her devotion to religion and her dedication to doing good. Regardless of where the people she meets are from, Yvonne Chiu treats each person with sincerity and kindness.

Generous donations born of love for humanity

Hanyu, a literatus from the Tang dynasty, wrote, "To possess universal love is to be benevolent, and to act on it is to be just." One of Yvonne Chiu's mottos in life has always been to "spare no effort in performing acts of kindness". She has helped the victims of the gas explosion in Kaohsiung in 2014, made the Modern Japanese Embroidery Exhibition featuring KusanoShizukapossible by sponsoring the event, made donations to the Nanshan Elementary School in Datong Village and students in the rural areas of Yilan County. In 2016, when Typhoon Nepartak wreaked havoc in Taitung, Yvonne Chiu led CISA in organizing the "0708 Fundraising Charity Event". She also extended a helping hand to victims of the major earthquake affecting Hualien in 2018.

Yvonne Chiu's compassion, born out of a strong humanitarian spirit, led her to put the needs of others before herself. Whenever she saw an opportunity for her to help other people, she would step up and rally her CISA members to donate generously to the cause, "We cannot let ourselves forget that our fellow citizens are suffering!" Even though Yvonne Chiu did not get any financial compensation for her work as the Chairperson and a board director of CISA, she would always fork out money from her own pocket to round up the donated amount without a moment's hesitation.

Volunteer work in India to eradicate polio

Yvonne Chiu has taken part in countless charity events, but the one that left the deepest impression on her was her End Polio trip to India. The gentle eyes of Yvonne Chiu bore the heartbreaking story that lent her strength and resolve those years ago.

"It was a charity event organized by the Rotary Club for members like us to go to India to provide humanitarian aid to end polio in the country. We came into contact with many children suffering from polio, and saw that their feet were deformed and appeared to be in different shapes — some were triangular, and some were round··· The Rotary Club members poured their hearts and souls into raising funds for these children to allow them to undergo restorative surgery, so that their feet can be normal once again." Yvonne Chiu let out a slow sigh at this point, hardly able to mask the sadness and pain in her voice.

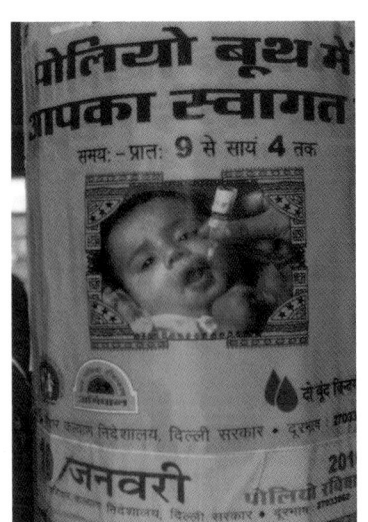

Posters put up in India to spread the word about the Rotary Club's End Polio Now campaign, which aims to eradicate polio around the world.

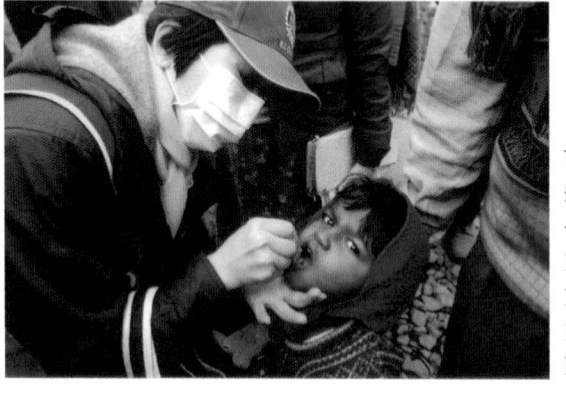

Yvonne Chiu, who is a huge fan of Bill Gates' humanitarian work, participated in the Rotary Club's End Polio Now campaign and went to India to learn about providing humanitarian aid.

"We participated in India's National Immunization Day (NID). As part of the program, we prepared a lot of gifts for the locals, including food and daily necessities. There were many people in the neighborhood, and we had to cover a lot of ground, so we marked each house after we visited them in order not to administer the treatment twice to each household. As the area under our charge was really huge, the Rotary Club volunteers decided to split up and divide the area into several districts. After we administered treatment to a child, we would make a mark on his or her nail and give him or her a gift. Those children were delighted to receive presents! What really broke my heart was that life in India was extremely tough, so some children resorted to scrapping off the marks on their nails just so that they could get a second gift···" Tears welled up in Yvonne Chiu's eyes even before she finished her sentence.

To help people, one has to TAKE ACTION!

"During the trip to India, we stayed in the slums, surrounded by garbage! The stench was so bad that it lingered on even after the trip. However, when I was there, I kept reminding myself that this is how those children live, and that thought gave me the motivation to keep going."

In that moment, the Chairperson of WITSA, a woman who has shaken the whole world, turned into a loving mother in the slums of India. She held back her tears and administered the treatment to the children one by one. "Seeing the children beg on the streets made me realize that shedding tears for them is pointless!" Her words rang out with conviction, for she saw how the children were trapped in a cycle of poverty. Try as they might, they could not escape their circumstances. The hardships that Yvonne Chiu bore witness to in India strengthened her resolve to do more for Taiwan.

Yvonne Chiu said, "In my speeches, I often share that if you wanted to do something well, first you have to make friends with the other party, and then execute the following steps: One, create awareness; two, lend a hand; three, take action; four, make dreams real." Yvonne Chiu's "protocol of success" helped her overcome challenges in her various pursuits. With her fists clenched and eyes shining with hope, she said, "I am confident that I can open new doors for Taiwan!"

Chapter Six

Becoming the Chairperson of WITSA

From CISA to WITSA
Connecting Taiwan with the World

The first Chairman of CISA

CISA was founded in 1983. In 2014, 12 years after Yvonne Chiu joined CISA and became an active member, she threw her name in to run as a candidate for the position of CISA Chairperson, with the support of CISA's Executive Supervisor. The election was set to take place in March, but Yvonne Chiu suffered an injury when playing golf in February. Everyone expected her to withdraw from the campaign due to her injury, but she stayed on in the race, even when wheelchair-bound. Due to her passion for her work and perseverance in her campaign, Yvonne Chiu successfully became the first Chairman of CISA in more than 30 years since its inception! As if her feat during the election was not impressive enough, she blew everybody's minds again during the Inauguration Ceremony in April. As the newly elected Chairperson, Yvonne Chiu wanted to show the other CISA members her determination to bring CISA to greater heights, and she epitomized this grit by grinding her teeth through the pain of a thousand needles from her injury. Yvonne Chiu got out of her wheelchair and took painful steps to the podium, supported by not crutches but her iron will. She even found the strength to laugh at herself, "They say 'the shell must break before the bird can fly.' I have no shell, but I guess bones count too, so I'm ready to soar!"

The ceremony took place in the Ambassador Hotel. Yvonne Chiu disclosed that the pain she felt from every step she took was so intense that she was close to fainting. It seemed like an eternity before she managed to grab hold of the podium. "I kept telling myself that, today, of all days, I could not admit defeat!" Yvonne Chiu's clothes were drenched with sweat by the time she made it on stage, but she hid her pain and put on a strong façade. With a radiant smile, she delivered her speech with gusto. Her rousing speech, combined with her impressive stance, won rounds of applause from all members of the audience! Yvonne Chiu has truly embodied the Hakka spirit of hard work and tenacity!

Ahead of one's time: Cross-industry collaboration

"When I was first elected as the CISA Chairperson, I had many curious questions directed my way, for instance, 'You understand the computer industry well, but do you really know the software industry?' In order to shut these doubters down, I spent the first four months of my time as the Chairperson learning everything about the software industry. Thereafter, I came up with a revolutionary paradigm that some would describe as avantgarde: Inter-industry, Inter-discipline, International!"

So, what does "inter-industry" refer to? It refers to the nature of the software industry to develop new products to cater to the different needs of different industries. What does "inter-discipline" mean in this context? It means that different fields of knowledge, for instance, design, engineering, medicine, architecture, software and hardware etc can all complement one another. What about "international"? When new software is launched, different countries pool resources to improve on it, so that advancements in technology can bring about the betterment of the entire human civilization! This is the direction in which the world is going, and Yvonne Chiu's perceptiveness of the trend led her to introduce a completely new and refreshing paradigm to the industry. Her revolutionary ideas have made Yvonne Chiu a household name in both the software and hardware industries in Taiwan!

● Boosting the software industry is a national effort

There were many misconceptions towards the software development industry in the eyes of the public. Hardware companies in Taiwan had huge factories and beautiful products that were known throughout the world. However, when it came to software development, both the quantity and the quality of the products from Taiwan did not seem to be picking up. Furthermore, there was a

mismatch between the size of the market and the industry's manpower needs. Business owners also found it hard to get funding to finance their business. Due to these circumstances, many software developers approached Yvonne Chiu for help. They hoped that she could speak to government agencies in the capacity of a representative from the software industry to ask for more support from the government. Yvonne Chiu lamented that many public servants were not far-sighted enough to appreciate the good that boosting the software industry could bring about for Taiwan, even after she spoke to relevant government officials. "After the millennium, Silicon Valley underwent a transformation, thanks to its software development stakeholders. In my opinion, there ought to be someone in the government who understands innovative industries such as the software industry, in order to tap on local demands and eventually expanding our reach to overseas markets. What Taiwan needed was not a 'pure software industry' like the one in the Silicon Valley but a 'software application' one. This is why I came up with an inter-industry and inter-discipline approach to growing the software industry. This approach would allow us to tap on the strengths of software experts as well as professionals in other fields in order to create a positive climate for developing software application tools that we can proudly call our own. I have faith, because Taiwan definitely has the means to achieve this goal!"

● Collaboration: Beginning from mutual understanding and ending in a win-win situation

After Yvonne Chiu became the CISA Chairperson, she was invited to speak at an event celebrating collaboration between Taiwan and Japan. In her speech, she shared her ideas about how to collaborate effectively using a long-term approach in order to achieve a win-win situation, "In the first year, we make friends; in the second, we take action; in the third, we make dreams come true!" Her approach, which was clearly not driven by a desire for short-term gains, earned the respect of the Japanese businessmen. There was once when the Vice President of Fujitsu gave a speech on stage and quoted these three statements, and he did not forget to credit Yvonne Chiu, "These three sentences come from Yvonne!"

The talent-spotting WITSA Ex-Chairman

In 2014, Yvonne Chiu, who was by then the Chairperson of CISA, flew to Guadalajara, Mexico, to attend the WCIT, a WITSA event. Yvonne Chiu went straight from the airport to the convention center, and she had a little shuteye at the convention center due to jetlag. She did not realize that the then-WITSA Chairman Sandiego, who was seeing her for the first time, had already taken note of this Asian lady whose petite frame did nothing to hide her strength.

After the two of them got acquainted with each other, Sandiego told Yvonne that when he saw her for the first time at the WCIT, he thought to himself, "I saw you. You are the one!" Yvonne Chiu, perplexed, asked him, "The one for what?" Sandiego then replied, "I wish to learn more about Taiwan's politics."

Yvonne Chiu, who had just taken up the position of CISA Chairperson, attends the 2014 WCIT in Guadalajara, Mexico.

Yvonne Chiu, who was always eager to help, immediately arranged for Sandiego to meet with Taiwanese politicians from various political parties.

When Sandiego met Joseph Wu, who was the Secretary-General of the Democratic Progressive Party cum chief representative of Taiwan to the United States, he told Joseph Wu unexpectedly, "She (Yvonne Chiu) would be a great candidate to run for the position of WITSA Chairperson." At that point, Yvonne Chiu thought that Sandiego was just joking. However, Joseph Wu, who had years of experience in the software industry and had also known Yvonne Chiu for years, agreed with Sandiego's idea immediately, "Definitely! I believe that with her as the WITSA Chairperson, it would be a great form of technology diplomacy!" It was then that Yvonne Chiu realized what Sandiego meant by "the one"!

With their support, Yvonne Chiu decided to fly to Canberra, Australia, in March 2015 to take part in the WITSA election. In the oath-taking ceremony before she left for Australia, Yvonne Chiu met with the then-Vice Premier of the Republic of China Simon Chang and received his full support. With the support of both the ruling party and the opposition, Yvonne Chiu decided to take the plunge.

Under the request of former WITSA Chairperson Sandiego (right), Yvonne Chiu for him to meet Joseph Wu, chief representative of Taiwan to the United States (left). At the meeting, they discussed future collaborations between Taiwan and WITSA as well as the issue of technology diplomacy.

Girl Power: Being elected as WITSA Chairperson

CISA Chairperson Yvonne Chiu, who had won the hosting rights for the 2017 WCIT, was on her way to becoming the Chairperson of WITSA, an international organization. What followed was a flurry of activities, including meeting WITSA members from all over the world, networking, and preparing for the election. On October 2, 2016, with the help of the former WITSA Chairperson, Yvonne Chiu successfully became the first Taiwanese person to assume the role of the Chairperson of WITSA, the biggest IT alliance in the world with over 83 countries as its members! Her victory in Brazil also represented another victory for Taiwan — Taiwan has finally gotten access to the United Nations!

Yvonne Chiu has visited more than 20 countries as the WITSA Chairperson. During her travels, she has met Presidents, Prime Ministers, Ministers, Commanders-in-Chief etc. "Many people whom I've met were surprised that I was Asian, and a woman⋯ I frequently remind myself that I have to work even harder, be more courageous, and not shy from difficulties. When it comes to problem-solving, I have to be more alert and react faster than the men." Yvonne Chiu rested her hands on the armrests of the sofa as she recounted the events of the past two years. Her secret to success has always been to be cautious and prudent. Her rise to the role of WITSA Chairperson marks the rise of "girl power" in the world, as well as the global community's recognition of Taiwan's status in the international IT industry.

On October 2, 2016, Yvonne Chiu successfully became the first Taiwanese person to become the Chairperson of WITSA, the biggest IT alliance in the world with over 83 countries as its members.

Taiwan won the rights to host the 2017 WCIT, thanks to Yvonne Chiu's strong campaign!

Amending WITSA charter for Taiwan to host WCIT

The Olympics of the IT world, WCIT, has always been a biannual event. Brazil was already set to host the 2016 WCIT, and four countries were vying for the chance to host the event in 2018. Hence, when Yvonne Chiu attended the WITSA convention in Guadalajara, Mexico, in 2014 for the first time as the Chairperson of CISA, she knew that at this rate, the earliest possible chance that Taiwan would only get to host the WCIT would be in 2020. The fast-thinking Yvonne Chiu came up with an idea on the spot which stunned everyone, "Technology is advancing all the time. As an international organization, WITSA should hold the WCIT yearly, so as to keep up with the times!" As soon as she finished, a thunderous applause rang out, and her proposal was taken up immediately by all present!

After Yvonne Chiu successfully convinced WITSA to amend its charter so that the WCIT can become a yearly event, the Secretary-general of WITSA suggested to Yvonne Chiu that Taiwan can host the 2019 WCIT, seeing how there were already four countries vying for the hosting rights of the 2018 WCIT. However, Yvonne Chiu was not easily convinced, "If Taiwan were to host the WCIT, it would have to be in 2017, for we have the full support of the government right now. Funding is not a problem!" Her words were the final push for WITSA to agree to let Taiwan host the 2017 WCIT.

In 2015, Yvonne Chiu met with Simon Chang, the former Premier of Taiwan (then Vice Premier), to get his support for the 2017 WCIT. Simon Chang was the CEO of Google's Asia operations and had vast knowledge and experience in business, public administration, and academia. He understood the importance of WCIT as well as its global impact, and knew that the chance for Taiwan to showcase its accomplishments and connect to the international community through this professional platform was priceless.

"WITSA is not a business association, and it is precisely because of its non-commercial nature that it provides the perfect platform for Taiwan to showcase our stellar accomplishments in the field of IT,"said the former Premier, "Hosting the WCIT will give Taiwan a voice on an international stage and increase Taiwan's visibility in the world. Thus, there was no reason for the government to say no!" Having received the full support of the then-Premier and various ministries, Yvonne Chiu shifted into top gear and flew many miles around the world, just so that the WCIT could bear sweet fruit!

Voice of Taiwan, solidarity of the nation

Former Premier of Taiwan Simon Chang was well aware of all the effort Yvonne Chiu has invested into the event. As the Chairperson of such a large international organization, the problems that Yvonne Chiu had to deal with were much more complex and trickier than the leader of a local organization, be it financial or professional issues, meeting the members' expectations, or handling interpersonal relationships across borders. "The road to happiness is strewn with setbacks. On top of the usual problems that a WCIT organizer might face, the preparation phase of the event coincided with the 2016 election in Taiwan." The former Premier pointed out, "Taiwan has very little maneuvering space internationally. There are certain things that the government is unable to do because of these political circumstances, but the people can step in and let the world know about important international conventions just like this one. This model proved successful, and can be adapted to other events organized by various non-governmental organizations."

Yvonne Chiu was immensely thankful for the support of Simon Chang, "Premier Chang was very generous; he asked me to write to then-President of Taiwan Ma Ying-jeou, in the hope that we can get the support of both incumbent and opposition parties for this event." Yvonne Chiu reiterated her point, "When Taiwan won the hosting rights for WCIT 2017, the international community was excited to see what Taiwan could do. To me, if we were to do something, we had to do it right. I would not allow Taiwan to become a laughing stock to the world!" Yvonne Chiu was faced with both time pressure and a myriad of uncertainties born out of multiple variables, but she pushed on and met with many government officials before finally getting the full support of Minister of Economic Affairs Shen Jong-chin. Once again, Yvonne Chiu had made a seemingly impossible task possible, thanks to her earnest and warm personality!

In 2015, Yvonne Chiu met with the then Premier of Taiwan Simon Chang to lobby for governmental support in her campaign to win the hosting rights of WCIT 2017. Simon Chang told Yvonne Chiu that the entire nation was behind her, and she had the support of both the government as well as the Taiwanese people. Taiwan is ready to show the world its prowess in the domain of technology!

WCIT 2017 @ Taiwan

In September 2017, Taiwan became the first country to host the WCIT in an odd-numbered year! Yvonne Chiu with President Tsai Ing-wen, Minister of Economic Affairs Shen Jong-chin, Wu Tsung-Tsong, and sponsors of the event.

In 2017, Taiwan became the first country to host the WCIT in an odd-numbered year!

In September 2017, the Olympics of the IT industry, the WCIT, returned to Taipei again after a hiatus of 17 years! Representatives of 83 countries attended the 21st WCIT. Guests from all over the world numbered in the thousands, and the event saw more than 4,500 world leaders in the IT field in attendance.

The Digital Dream exposition that took place at Expo Hall 1 opened its doors to the public on September 10, 2017. This futuristic exhibition showcasing state of the art technology at over 680 booths was made possible because of

Kyoko Yoshihiro, Chairman of USE, a Japanese company, flew to Taiwan specially for the WCIT. She had a lively discussion with Yvonne Chiu about the future of digital technology.

the collaborative effort of industry players, government agencies, academic institutions, and R&D organizations, with the goal of providing a platform for international B2B networking. For the next three days, 16 concurrent conferences and events were held in the Taipei International Convention Center (TICC), during which the participants shared their visions of digital dreams of the future.

Minister of Economic Affairs Shen Jong-chin pointed out that the WCIT 2017 was more than a three-day international convention. More importantly, it was a great opportunity for the world to get to know the applications of technology in our smart nation. Local exhibitors at the event included both established major companies and startups, and the profile of these companies was a strong indication of Taiwan's evolution from a nation powered by its OEM industry to one that has a strong expertise in its application of IT services. The maturation of Taiwan's IT industry provided positive boosts to both our society and economy.

Premier William Lai (third from left) and leaders from various sectors extended an invitation to IT professionals around the world to join Taiwan in the growth of its digital economy.

Premier of the Republic of China William Lai stated during theWCIT dinner that Taiwan has set a course for its national development, which is to shift its focus from manufacturing and OEM to developing smart technologies and innovative products. Taiwan aims to be a leader in areas such as developing a digital economy, the Internet of Things, big data analysis, cloud computing, artificial intelligence etc.

Closing the digital gap: From Taiwan to the world

The three-day event officially commenced on the 11th of September. President Tsai Ing-wen, Minister without Portfolio of Executive Yuan Wu Tsung-tsong, Minister of Economic Affairs Shen Jong-chin, Mayor of Taipei Ko Wen-je, as well as WITSA Chairperson Yvonne Chiu spoke at the WCIT 2017 Opening Ceremony to welcome more than 4,000 esteemed guests from 83 countries around the world to the convention.

As the WITSA Chairperson, Yvonne Chiu delivered an English speech in front of her international audience. She stressed the importance of this approach, "WITSA members came from 82[5] different countries, and they are the cream of the crop in the international IT community. Making my speech in English was a statement to the world that Taiwan was more than ready to join the rest of the world on international platforms!" As such, the Mama Chiu who started out on her journey by connecting young people from Xizhi to the world in 1996 has, by remaining true to herself over the past 20 years, become the catalyst to effect change in Taiwan and connect Taiwan to these 83 other nations!

Yvonne Chiu has single-handedly revolutionized Taiwan's IT industry and connected Taiwan to the world and also put forth her idea to "level the global digital playing field in order for all to become digital global citizens". Looking back on WITSA Chairperson Yvonne Chiu's past, it was clear that she never wavered from her course. Yvonne Chiu, modest as ever, said simply that all the work she had done was a mission given to her by the divine powers.

"20 years ago, my hope was to 'level the digital playing field' in Taiwan; 20 years on, I am still doing pretty much the same thing, except that I now want to widen the scope of my work so that I can not only help Taiwan

achieve this goal, but also the rest of the world!" With her unrelenting ambition, Yvonne Chiu marched towards the United Nations, a Taiwanese superwoman ready to take on the world!

---

[5] As of August 22, 2018, Bhutan has become the 83rd country to join the WITSA.

The phoenix takes flight

Onwards, to the United Nations

Fighting for a place for Taiwan:WITSA Chairman in the UN

"The WITSA Secretary-General and I came up with the slogan 'Living the Digital Dream' for the WCIT after much discussion. It is also a dream that I aspire towards!" Yvonne Chiu's gaze was faraway as she reminisced.

In the spring of 2017, Yvonne Chiu attended the United Nations Conference on Trade and Development (UNCTAD) in the capacity of the WITSA Chairperson. She saw that representatives from various countries were holding their respective national flags, but Taiwan's flag was nowhere to be seen in that sea of flags. Just then, someone approached Yvonne Chiu and asked, "Where do you come from?" Yvonne Chiu then answered in a clear voice, "Taiwan!" That person was taken aback, and he tried to wave her away, saying, "You can't be here!" Yvonne Chiu showed him her name card and explained, "I'm the Chairperson of WITSA!" The other party did not expect that the Taiwanese lady in front of him held the important role of being the Chairperson of WITSA, the largest IT alliance internationally. He apologized profusely and immediately ushered her to her seat, "Your seat is over here!" After she was seated, Yvonne Chiu could not help but lament the helplessness of Taiwan in international settings. Thus, Yvonne Chiu looked at the WITSA Chairperson tag in front of her and resolved to connect Taiwan to the world!

The conference was being held in the Headquarters of the United Nations, and there were two other events going on at the same time in the building – a Chinese art exhibition and Jack Ma's press conference. Jack Ma's confidence and self-possession was a stark contrast to the slight that Yvonne Chiu had just been put through. She lamented Taiwan's position, "A bottom-up approach does not suffice to elevate Taiwan's standing in the world. To secure a brighter future for Taiwan, we have to grow as anation!" Yvonne Chiu, who had single-handedly overcome numerous obstacles to garner support for her cause and achieved what

Yvonne Chiu attends the UNCTAD conference in 2017.

few could claim to have accomplished, clenched her fists in determination. The sparkle in her eyes was a testament to her conviction. Yvonne Chiu, a fighter born and bred in Taiwan, pushed through various forms of resistance and emerged stronger every time, incessantly working to open new doors for her homeland in order to connect Taiwan with the world.

Long since a Taiwanese representative attended a United Nations Breakfast Meeting

Dr. Jim Poisant, long-time Secretary-General of WITSA, was also with Yvonne Chiu at the conference. Having attended several UN events, Dr. Poisant was a familiar face to many attendees of the conference and was thus invited to the breakfast meeting the following morning. UN breakfast meetings are held on the top floor of the UN Headquarters and are highly exclusive, counting only the most important conference attendees as its guests. Dr. Poisant invited Yvonne Chiu to attend the breakfast meeting with him, for the meeting was a great opportunity for Yvonne Chiu to meet with big-league players around the world.

At the breakfast meeting, Yvonne Chiu introduced herself, "I'm WITSA's Chairperson. I'm from Taiwan." She extended an invitation to the Secretary-General of UNCTAD for him to speak in Taiwan, telling him that Taiwan possesses a lot of IT talents and resources that can be tapped on to help other countries in need. However, she realized that a sense of uneasiness rippled out whenever she mentioned the word "Taiwan". Even before she was done speaking, she was rudely interrupted, "We belong to the United Nations."

Upon hearing this, the ever-candid Yvonne Chiu replied without the slightest hesitation, never mind that she was in the UN Headquarters there and then, "Forget about the politics, we are in the industry!" She then went on to share about the Institute for Information Industry in the capacity of the Institute's Managing Director, and was validated by a representative from another country, who had received help from the Institute for Information Industry earlier. "I mentioned 'Taiwan' a few times, but was met with silence…" Yvonne Chiu choked on her words. It was evident that she, who always wears her heart on her sleeve, was pained by that memory, "Many people do not know this, but Taiwan really has a hard time when it comes to international affairs…" Yvonne Chiu tilted her head back, hiding the tears welling up in her eyes.

Taking flight: Daughter of Taiwan

The WCIT 2017 came to a close after a successful execution, and Yvonne Chiu was invited to Mexico by a Mexican minister to be a prize presenter at the awards ceremony. In Mexico, Yvonne Chiu was featured on the newspapers. The Mexican press wanted its people to know this Taiwanese lady who is the Chairperson of WITSA, and who successfully organized WCIT 2017, the Olympics of the IT world!

In February 2018, Yvonne Chiu flew to India for a WITSA board meeting. As the international Chairperson of WITSA, Yvonne Chiu shared about the Smart City initiative by the Taipei Computer Association and invited all WITSA members to attend the event in Taiwan. Furthermore, within a month, she

Yvonne Chiu was invited to visit Mexico in 2017. Yvonne Chiu with Gerardo Ruiz Esparza, Minister of Transport in Mexico (second from right).

Yvonne Chiu was invited to speak in India in February 2018. Yvonne Chiu with Sadhguru (second from left).Sadhguru is among the top 100 influential figures in India, and is a spirituality guru known throughout the world.

Yvonne Chiu with K.T. Rama Rao, Minister for Information Technology in Telangana, India (second from right) and NASSCOM President RentalaChandrashekhar(first from right) in January2018. Yvonne Chiu faciliated the signing of a MOU between Taoyuan and Hyderabad, an Indian city known for its outstanding IT industry.

Yvonne Chiu takes a picture before the breakfast meeting of the United Nations Economics Roundtable session, held at Geneva, Switzerland, in April 2018.

faciliated the signing of a MOU between Taoyuan and Hyderabad, an Indian city known for its outstanding IT industry, bringing about inter-city diplomacy as a form of expedited international diplomacy.

Fast forward to April 2018, Yvonne Chiu participated in the United Nations Economics Roundtable session held in Geneva, Switzerland, and was invited to the UN breakfast meeting for the second time. Yvonne Chiu smiled and said that she was more relaxed this time round, for she had already met with some of the guests at the previous breakfast meeting. Later on, when the Deputy Chairperson of WTO's Taiwan office got to know about her attendance at the breakfast meeting, he asked Yvonne Chiu in surprise, "You're really something! How did you get yourself into that breakfast meeting?" By then, Yvonne Chiu had already made many friends in the UN. She replied with a smile, "Good thing that I am the WITSA Chairperson, or else I wouldn't even have been allowed to set foot in the UN Headquarters!"

In May 2018, Yvonne Chiu was invited to the Federation of Hellenic Information Technology & Communications Enterprises (SEPE), organized by Greece, also a WITSA member nation. She attended the Digital Economy Forum in Athens, Greece, where she spoke of the importance of ICT as a driving force of the global economy, and how governments that understand this phenomenon ought to base all policies and decision-making processes on developments in ICT technologies. Yvonne Chiu also pointed out that the mission of WITSA is "Fulfilling the Promise of the Digital Age", and so she hoped that every life around the world would be bettered by advancements in the ICT field. Yvonne Chiu's grand vision for international development won her a thunderous round of applause which did not abate for a long time.

Besides speaking at the Digital Economy Forum, Yvonne Chiu also invited Kuo Shih-nan, Taiwan's top envoy to Greece, to the Digital Economy Forum gala dinner, where he met with Alexis Tsipras, the Prime Minister of Greece.

Yvonne Chiu takes a picture before the breakfast meeting of the United Nations Economics Roundtable session, held at Geneva, Switzerland, in April 2018.

Kuo Shih-nan shared Taiwan's accomplishments in the ICT field with Alexis Tsipras and expressed his hopes that Taiwan and Greece would have more opportunities to work together to help each other grow economically.

Yvonne Chiu then went to Armenia to meet with the newly-elected Prime Minister of Armenia NikolPashinyan, who had just been sworn into office in May 2018. After leading a non-violent revolution in Armenia, Pashinyan became the country's Prime Minister. Shortly after taking office, Pashinyan met with Russian President Vladimir Putin. Upon his return to Armenia, the first foreign guests he received were representatives of WITSA, namely its Chairman Yvonne Chiu, Secretar General Dr. Jim Poisant, and Chief Strategy Officer of WITSA Asia Representative Office Suzzan Tsai. During the meeting, the new Armenian Prime Minister stressed repeatedly that digital technology would be at the heart of Armenia's transformation. He also enlisted Yvonne Chiu as his advisor in the

Yvonne Chiu meets with the newly-elected Armenian Prime MinisterNikolPashinyan in Armenia in May 2018. At the meeting, they discussed technological developments at the national level.

Yvonne Chiu also meets with ArmenSarkissian, President of Armenia, on the same trip. They exchanged their thoughts on possible future collaborations in the area of ICT between Taiwan and Armenia.

hope that Armenia would, like Taiwan, become recognized as a leading force in the international IT industry, after the nation hosts a successful WCIT 2019.

In July 2018, Yvonne Chiu was invited to speak at the Singapore World Blockchain Conference. The theme of the conference was "Next in Blockchain", and it sought to explore future international developments and applications of blockchain technology. During her speech, Yvonne Chiu talked about how Taiwan was helping Estonia in terms of the application of blockchain technology, and how Estonia has successfully transformed into an exemplar of a digital nation through the establishment of an electronic taxation system, electronic electoral system, digitized healthcare records, and so on. She also shared that Taiwan has applied blockchain technology to areas such as finance, medicine, supply chain management, energy trading and management of supply and demand, agriculture, digital rights managements, and public management etc, with impressive results. She expressed her hope that Taiwan would have more opportunities to work closely with various countries around the world as blockchain technology grows and matures.

Regardless whether she was in Mexico, India, Greece, Thailand, or in Singapore, Yvonne Chiu would always adopt the same approach – opening doors as a civil representative and simultaneously connecting government officials. With her entourage of Taiwanese representatives posted to various countries, Yvonne Chiu would set up meetings with local government officials. This way, diplomats from Taiwan, who had long been denied these meetings, would finally get the chance to meet high-ranking government officials in these countries. Little wonder that Taiwanese diplomats were all delighted whenever they hear that Yvonne Chiu was in town!

"I often thought about this, that if the G20 summit could bring together different countries to discuss issues pertaining to the global economy, what could an ICT20 summit achieve? Such an alliance will prove vital internationally. 83 nations are members of WITSA, which means that there are 83 chances for Taiwan to work with these countries in 'non-official ways'. Eventually, Taiwan can become the heart of the international ICT industry, and at the same time build stronger and deeper diplomatic ties with these countries through our collaborations."

Soft Power is changing the world

It would be an understatement to say that Yvonne Chiu understands the pressure that women face in the workplace. On the surface, Yvonne Chiu's career was smooth sailing, but she was no stranger to such pressures. In 2017 alone, she had to undergo a fair share of oppression and discrimination when she was running for her second term as the Chairman of CISA. "At that time, virtually all of my friends, , including top businessmen, advised me against running for that position a second time! What's more, an old friend who had worked with me for more than 10 years talked to me over the phone for over an hour just to persuade me not to try for a second term!"

In the face of the overwhelming pressure she faced, Yvonne Chiu had only one reply for her doubters, "I, Yvonne Chiu, hold my own future in my own hands!"

"Perhaps, this trait is part of my nature, this… resilience." Even though Yvonne Chiu stated that with a gentle smile, the tenacity in her eyes could not be missed. "Back when I was running a business in the United States, I tried ways and means to solve any problem that came my way, and refused to give up until I achieved my goal. Later on, I became the Chairman of both CISA and WITSA. In these positions, I met with countless problems, but I stuck to my stubbornness and pushed through all of these obstacles. My doctor told me that I needed to learn to take breaks and relax, and I replied that I do know how to relieve my stress. To me, the best way to release tension is to live in the moment and make the best of our lives!"

Despite her position as the international Chairman of WITSA, Yvonne Chiu was still adamant that she ran her own household. Whenever she finds time from her busy schedule, she would visit the local market and make a hearty meal for her family, who especially love her signature dishes, pasta and grilled

steak! "I constantly remind myself that I have to learn to do everything myself if I wished to become even better. If other people can do something, there is no reason why I can't!" Yvonne Chiu, who has helped improve computer education in Taiwan, contributed to the increased employment of women in the work force, and also been passionate in her charity work, firmly believes that "Soft power is changing the world!"

Yvonne Chiu has shared her forward-looking vision of "Digital Prowess as National Prowess, Cybersecurity as National Security" with President Tsai Ing-wen in person, and also discussed both the opportunities and obstacles of Taiwan-US diplomatic relations with Hillary Clinton, the US' Democratic Party's nominee for President of the United States. Yvonne Chiu stated, "When we talk about 'Girl Power' today, we mean a tenacity and grit that carries us to our goals. A woman's determination can transform the world!"

Yvonne Chiu shared her vision "Digital Prowess as National Prowess, Cybersecurity as National Security" with President Tsai Ing-wen in person.

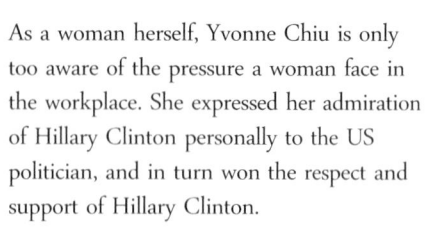

As a woman herself, Yvonne Chiu is only too aware of the pressure a woman face in the workplace. She expressed her admiration of Hillary Clinton personally to the US politician, and in turn won the respect and support of Hillary Clinton.

When Yvonne isasked, "Why do you work so hard?"

She would reply, "I work hard for my mother."

"Who is your mother?"

"My mother, is Taiwan."

2018 Digital Economy Forum—WITSA Chairman's Keynote Address

（2018數位經濟論壇—WITSA邱月香主席致詞稿）

時間：2018.05.07　地點：希臘雅典 (Athens, Greece)

Good Morning Excellency, distinguished guests, ladies and gentlemen. On behalf of the World Information Technology & Services Alliance (WITSA), it is my honor to join you today at SEPE's Digital Economy Forum.

For those of you who may not be familiar with WITSA, WITSA is a consortium of leading Information and Communication Technology Associations with 83 country members-representing over 90% of the ICT industry—the most comprehensive and influential entity representing the ICT and services industry around the world. SEPE of course is WITSA's member from Greece. I would especially like to thank SEPE's Director General, Mr. Yannis Sirros for his friendship, as well as SEPE's long-time support of WITSA. I would also like to congratulate SEPE and all of Greece on the many WITSA Global ICT Excellence awards you have won over the years. As a testament to its innovative and robust ICT sector, Greece has often been recognized through WITSA's award program.

It is important as I begin my remarks, that I mention WITSA's vision as it key to understanding WITSA's global role. WITSA's vision is to Fulfill the Promise of the Digital Age. In other words, our job will not be completed until every person on earth is benefiting from Information and Communication technology.

Information & Communication Technologies is the key driver of the global economy. Governments that recognize this fact must consider ICT as the core of all decision making. There is global competition among countries. Therefore, there is great danger of falling behind and conversely great benefits from leading.

Since the mid-1990s, the Digital Age or the Information or Knowledge Age, has had and continues to have a massively transformative impact on cultures, societies, commerce, and technology; including the rise of near-instant communication by electronic means, instant messaging, voice over Internet Protocol, interactive video calls, Internet discussion fora, blogs, social networking and e-Commerce. To provide you with a vivid example of the power and impact of the Digital Age, according to the United Nations Conference on Trade and Development (UNCTAD) the Global E-Commerce market in 2018 is estimated to be worth $22 trillion US dollars.

In addition to affecting nearly every aspect of human life, the Digital Age continues to evolve in the areas of Artificial Intelligence, Nano Technology, 3D Printing, Block chain Technology, Big Data, Machine Learning, autonomous transportation, robotics and the Internet of Things.

The Digital Age is in the midst of totally transforming the public and private sectors to include the Financial, Entertainment, Transportation, Agriculture, Manufacturing, Defense, Communications, Education and the Health Care industries as well as Governments at all levels.

For those of us in the ICT industry we face a particular dilemma. Due to the extensive use of ICT by our customers, they are adopting to new technology at a rapid pace. This means we need to stay in front of the technology trends in order to continue to provide value to our customers. ICT companies either have to reinvent themselves or figure out a way to continue to add value to their customers.

Here is an example, MasterCard operates Bank net, a global telecommunications network linking all MasterCard card issuers, acquirers, and data processing centers into a single financial network. Instead of Master Card considering itself in the Credit Card business they think of themselves as being in the Information & Communications Technology business. As Master Card has transformed itself, so must all businesses; especially the ones that have existed for a long time. It is true today more than any time in the past, that companies that do not transform and adapt to the Digital Age will no longer exist.

It is encouraging to read that Nikos Pappas, Minister of Digital Policy, Telecommunications and Media is working with industry and being a major driver of Greece's technological revolution. As your revolution continues to grow, so too will the many benefits it will provide to your wonderful country. WITSA fully endorses all of your efforts to establish Greece as a Digital nation and regional hub.

As Greece continues to transform and grow, efforts should be redoubled to ensure benefits are reaped by all your citizens, across all economic, socio-demographic and geographic strata. No one should be left behind in the Digital Age both from an economic as well as social perspective.

As we reflect on the breathtaking changes and benefits continually being gained from the Digital Age, we (all stakeholders), face three (3) critical challenges as we look toward the future of the Digital Age:

1. The benefits of the Digital Age are not being shared with nearly half the world's population, nor is there a guarantee they will ever be included.

2. The evolution of the Digital Age is at a critical juncture in its development. The Digital Age is in its infancy and as an infant, this new age faces a number of significant challenges if it is to survive and flourish.

3. Actions taken by all stakeholders at this point in time, will determine the future of the Digital Age.

In order to continue the astonishing and beneficial growth of ICT, number of key factors need to be in place:

An impartial regulatory environment needs to be established that promotes Digital technologies,

Reliable and affordable infrastructure must be offered to everyone,

Public-private partnerships that promote entrepreneurship and innovation need to be established and promoted,

A competitive environment by reducing barriers to entry of products, services and talent;

Policy interventions that discourages innovators and new competitive business models should be avoided;

Fostering a Risk-Enabled Culture is critically important. Countries interested in fostering innovations need to understand that innovations depend on a number of factors to include instilling a culture which recognizes that failure is most times a prerequisite to success-not a career-ending endeavor. In an ideal innovation ecosystem, entrepreneurship is encouraged, failure is accepted, finances are available, mentorships are employed and educational and business resources are in place;

Public-Private partnerships need to exist in all aspects of government planning, at all levels;

Global open technical standards need to be established, agreed upon and adhered to,

The Digital Age must provide all citizens with the right of privacy and trust;

Intellectual property must be protected;

A principled approach to privacy, security and data protection which instills trust and confidence in the fundamental building blocks of the Digital Age,

Transparent access to new and existing technologies,

A free flow of data and talent across borders,

Having a digitally skilled domestic workforce,

As we know, there are complex factors in meeting each one of these challenges. Governments struggle with resource allocations based on real-time, pressing societal needs.

However, it is proven that those countries that do make the decision to commit to ICT development benefit greatly from their decision.

Governments needs to have long-term strategic Digital agendas or plans that plot and oversee the roll out of digital applications and benefits. I stress long-term plans because National Agendas must not be weakened or discarded

during changes in government leadership. Once again, this need to be done in partnership with the ICT Industry. I would like to commend Greece on your National Digital Strategy Initiative. Please stay on course over the long term.

The Digital Age has always been and continues to be driven by INNOVATION. Innovation is most often created by small & medium sized enterprises. To fully cover the subject of INNOVATION would take much longer than the time we have today. However, I would like to share my thoughts with you from 1st hand experience in Taiwan. If I had to choose the most important factor in establishing new companies and innovation, it would have to be the Taiwan governments and Taiwan ICT industry' commitment to fostering new ideas and companies.

In order for the vast majority of small businesses to flourish they need resources and support from governments. They need experienced, proven business mentors to guide them from the ICT industry. It is when the government and ICT industry closely cooperate, that innovations will emerge. For those of you who wish to learn more about how a small island became a global ICT powerhouse please let me know. Please also see our policy papers posted on the WITSA web site.

I would like to leave you with an observation and a recommendation. My observation is the main ICT platforms, markets such as computer operating systems are already mature. Chances are, if you spend your time and resources in markets dominated by already mature technologies and applications, you will more than likely fail. On the other hand, if you focus your attention in your local community you will find many opportunities to serve new customers. More than likely your innovations would be scalable globally.

Once again, thank you for kind attention. I wish you well with your conference and your commitment to be among the leaders in the Digital Age.

2018 ASOCIO Plenary Meeting & 3rd Bhutan International Training Event—WITSA Chairman's Keynote Address

（第三屆不丹國際信息技術與培訓活動–WITSA邱月香主席致詞稿）

時間：2018.06.21　地點：不丹廷布（Thimphu, Bhutan）

Good Morning Excellency, distinguished guests, ladies and gentlemen. On behalf of the World Information Technology & Services Alliance (WITSA), it is my honor to join you today at the 3rd Bhutan International IT & Training Event.

For those of you who may not be familiar with WITSA, WITSA is a consortium of leading Information and Communication Technology Associations with 83 country members-representing over 90% of the ICT industry—the most comprehensive and influentialentity representing the ICT and services industry around the world.

I would especially like to thank the Bhutan ICT & Training Association and, in particular, President Phub Gyeltshen & Secretary General Kiran Parajuli for this invitation and opportunity. Information & Communication Technologies is the key driver of the global economy.

Governments that recognize this fact must consider ICT as the core of all decision making.

There is global competition among countries. Therefore, there is great danger of falling behind andconversely great benefits from leading.

Since the mid-1990s, the Digital Age has had and continues to have a massively transformative impact on cultures, societies, commerce, and technology; including the rise of near-instant communication by electronic means, instant messaging, voice over Internet Protocol, interactive video calls, Internet discussion fora, blogs, social networking and e-Commerce.

To provide you with a vivid example of the power and impact of the Digital Age, according to the United Nations Conference on Trade and Development (UNCTAD) the Global E-Commerce market in 2018 is estimated to be worth $22 trillion US dollars.

In addition to affecting nearly every aspect of human life, the Digital Age continues to evolve in the areas of Artificial Intelligence, Nano Technology, 3D Printing, Blockchain Technology, Big Data, Machine Learning, autonomous transportation, robotics and the Internet of Things.

The Digital Age is in the midst of totally transforming the public and private sectors to include the Financial, Entertainment, Transportation, Agriculture, Manufacturing, Defense, Communications, Education and the Health Care industries as well as Governments at all levels.

For those of us in the ICT industry we face a particular dilemma. Due to the extensive use of ICT by our customers, they are adopting to new technology at a rapid pace.

This means we need to stay in front of the technology trends in order to continue to provide value to our customers.

ICT companies either have to reinvent themselves or figure out a way to continue to add value to their customers. Here is an example, MasterCard operates Banknet, a global telecommunications network linking all MasterCard card issuers, acquirers, and data processing centers into a single financial network.

Instead of MasterCard considering itself in the Credit Card business they think of themselves as being in the Information & Communications Technology business. As MasterCard has transformed itself, so must all businesses; especially the ones that have existed for a long time.

It is true today more than any time in the past, that companies that do not transform and adapt to the Digital Age will no longer exist.

Bhutan seen significant improvements in its ICT sector in recent years, in particular with regard to mobile phone connectivity and broadband, and its

ranking in ITU's ICT development index has improved from 122nd to 117th in the span of just one year.

No doubt, this in part due to the Bhutan government's efforts to adopt ICT as a top priority, and its willingness to work with BICTTA and the ICT industry in developing a framework for growth and development and driving Bhutan's technological revolution. WITSA applauds Bhutan's enthusiastic adoption of the Bhutan ICT Roadmap and Bhutan E-Government Masterplan, which seek to use ICT to improve its services to its citizens.

As noted by The World Bank in the 2016 World Development Report on "Digital Dividends", Bhutan's adoption of digital technologies has boosted growth, expanded opportunities, and improved service delivery.

As your digital revolution continues to grow, so, too will the many benefits it will provide to your wonderful country.

WITSA fully endorses all of your efforts to establish Bhutan as a Digital nation and regional hub. As Bhutan continues to transform and grow, efforts should be redoubled to ensure benefits are reaped by all your citizens, across all economic, socio-demographic and geographic strata. No one should be left behind in the Digital Age both from an economic as well as social perspective.

As we reflect on the breathtaking changes and benefits continually being gained from the Digital Age, we (all stakeholders), face three (3) critical challenges as we look toward the future of the Digital Age:

1. The benefits of the Digital Age are not being shared with nearly half the world' population, nor is there a guarantee they will ever be included.

2. The evolution of the Digital Age is at a critical juncture in its development. The Digital Age is in its infancy and as an infant, this new age faces a number of significant challenges if it is to survive and flourish.

3. Actions taken by all stakeholders at this point in time, will determine the future of the Digital Age.

In order to continue the astonishing and beneficial growth of ICT, number of

key factors need to be in place:

An impartial regulatory environment needs to be established that promotes Digital technologies,

Reliable and affordable infrastructure must be offered to everyone,

Public-private partnerships that promote entrepreneurship and innovation need to be established and promoted,

A competitive environment by reducing barriers to entry of products, services and talent;

Policy interventions that discourages innovators and new competitive business models should be avoided;

Fostering a Risk-Enabled Culture is critically important. Countries interested in fostering innovations need to understand that innovations depend on a number of factors to include instilling a culture which recognizes that failure is most times a prerequisite to success-not a career-ending endeavor. In an ideal innovation ecosystem, entrepreneurship is encouraged, failure is accepted, finances are available, mentorships are employed and educational and business resources are in place;

Public-Private partnerships need to exist in all aspects of government planning, at all levels;

Global open technical standards need to be established, agreed upon and adhered to,

The Digital Age must provide all citizens with the right of privacy and trust;

Intellectual property must be protected;

A principled approach to privacy, security and data protection which instills trust and confidence in the fundamental building blocks of the Digital Age,

Transparent access to new and existing technologies,

A free flow of data and talent across borders,

Having a digitally skilled domestic workforce,

As we know, there are complex factors in meeting each one of these challenges. Governments struggle with resource allocations based on real-time, pressing societal needs.

However, it is proven that those countries that do make the decision to commit to ICT development benefit greatly from their decision. Governments needs to have long-term strategic Digital agendas or plans that plot and oversee the roll out of digital applications and benefits.

I stress long-term plans because National Agendas must not be weakened or discarded during changes in government leadership.

Once again, this need to be done in partnership with the ICT Industry. I would like to commend Bhutan on your Bhutan ICT Roadmap. Please stay on course over the long term.

The Digital Age has always been and continues to be driven by INNOVATION.

Innovation is most often created by small & medium sized enterprises. To fully cover the subject of INNOVATION, would take much longer than the time we have today.

However, I would like to share my thoughts with you from 1st hand experience in Taiwan. If I had to choose the most important factor in establishing new companies and innovation, it would have to be the Taiwan governments and Taiwan's ICT industry's commitment to fostering new ideas and companies.

In order for the vast majority of small businesses to flourish they need resources and support from governments. They need experienced, proven business mentors to guide them from the ICT industry.

It is when the government and ICT industry closely cooperate, that innovations will emerge.

For those of you who wish to learn more about how a small island became a global ICT powerhouse please let me know. Please also see our policy papers

posted on the WITSA web site.

I would like to leave you with an observation and a recommendation. My observation is the main ICT platforms, markets such as computer operating systems are already mature. Chances are, if you spend your time and resources in markets dominated by already mature technologies and applications, you will more than likely fail.

On the other hand, if you focus your attention in your local community you will find many opportunities to serve new customers. More than likely your innovations would be scalable globally.

Once again, thank you for kind attention.

I wish well with your conference and commitment to be among the leader in the Digital Age.

Thank you.

Singapore World Blockchain Conference—WITSA Chairman's Keynote Address

（新加坡世界區塊鏈峰會—WITSA邱月香主席致詞稿）

時間：2018.07.17　地點：新加坡泛太平洋酒店（Pan Pacific Singapore）

Good morning your excellencies, distinguished guests, ladies and gentlemen. I am the chairman of WITSA and CISA.

For those who may not be familiar with the World Information Technology and Services Alliance (WITSA), please allow me to say that WITSA is a consortium of leading Information and Communication Technology Associations.

WITSA members represent 82 countries and economies. Of course, SG Tech is WITSA's member in Singapore. CISA is a software association of Taiwan.

As you know, Blockchain technology is receiving wide spread acclaim-predicted as a revolutionary technology that is changing the world. Time will tell if all of the predictions will come true; however, from WITSA's perspective, it most certainly will make an enormous impact on many people throughout the world who desperately need to realize its benefits.

Before I describe the a few ways Block Chain technology will affect those most in need, I would like to mention that WITSA, even though we represent over 90% of the ICT industry around the globe, has a that vision extends much wider than our industry.

WITSA's vision is Fulfilling the Promise of the Digital Age. In other words, WITSA's job will be completed when every person on earth enjoys the benefits of ICTs.

When every child on earth has access to libraries of information. When needless loss of life and suffering are eliminated by health and safety benefits

enabled by ICTs.

As we see it, Block Chain Technology is an enabling technology that fits beautifully into WITSA's vision. Let's take a look at how. As I mentioned in my brief opening remarks, due to Blockchain technology a land owner does not need to fear losing his or her land because the deed for their land cannot be stolen or changed.

Let's not stop at one deed contracts—let's expand Block Chain to all contracts and agreements that are susceptible to fraud. In the area of Heath Care, Blockchain technology offers a distributed framework to improve the integration of health care information for all stakeholders.

It provides a more secure, efficient and trusted health care system. Everyone can benefit here, if there is nationwide interoperability. Current technologies do not fully address these requirements, since they are limited in the areas of privacy, security and interoperability.

As we know, current health care records are disjointed due to the lack of common architectures. If the full benefits of Blockchain Technology in Healthcare are to be realized there is much to do.

In the area of Global Food Supplies, a recent study estimates that as much as 50 percent of all food produced is thrown away in the United States alone. Even though, theoretically, the world generates enough food to feed everyone, 842 million people suffer from hunger worldwide.

One up and coming company called FoodCoin Ecosystem which is based on Blockchain technology, has designed and created a global marketplace for food and agricultural products. The system is intended to provide food for millions of people. This solution, together with other new Block Chain applications have an enormous potential; especially among the poor.

These are but a few examples; however, be assured that BlockChain technology has the potential of impacting every aspect of our societies. I would now like to take this opportunity to share with you how my country—Taiwan is

engaging in Blockchain Technology.

Taiwan blockchain applications include but a not limited to:

Digital currency, bank cross-border payment and remittance, e-ticket and crowdfunding in the financial sector.

Applications extend into medical care (Electronic medical records), drug development,

Supply chain management

Energy trading, energy supply and demand management,

Agriculture (such as food production and sales, food safety),

Digital copyright (such as copyright authorization, artwork Authenticity identification)

Public management (such as electronic voting, identity authentication).

All of the above services require a good technical team, but not every company can have such a technical team, and CISA has a committee to research and improving technology to solve this problem and we have the first leader in the Taiwan public sidechain technology.

As blockchain applications are emerging and involve cross-disciplinary and cross-border cooperation, they require a very close connection and partnership between the ICT industry and governments.

In my opinion, Blockchain technology holds enormous potential and promise to change the world BUT ONLY if all the major stakeholders work together to make it happen.

Thank you very much for your kind attention. Please enjoy the event. Wish you good wealth, good health and world peace. I love Singapore!